THE ORTHODOX CHURCH

A WELL-KEPT SECRET

A JOURNEY THROUGH CHURCH HISTORY

By Father George Nicozisin

LIGHT & LIFE PUBLISHING
Minneapolis, Minnesota

Light and Life Publishing
P.O. Box 26421
Minneapolis, Minnesota 55426-0421

Library of Congress Card No. 97-74585

ISBN 1-880971-33-X

AUTHOR"S PREFACE

"The Orthodox Church: A Well-kept Secret" was written for older Sunday School Classes, Christian education for adults and a catechism for potential converts to the Orthodox Christian Faith. A little Old Testament background is given to lay the foundation for the Coming of Jesus Christ. New Testament and Apostolic Times are touched upon to introduce the beginning of the Christian Church. The Development of the Christian Church, the emergence of Papal Authority, the Great Schism (1054), the Four Crusades (1095-1261), the Fall of Constantinople (1453), the Protestant Reformation (1517), the English Reformation (1534), the Calvanist Movement (1541), the Greek Revolution (1821), the emergence of Orthodox Christianity on the American Continent (1794), the Protestant Churches today, the Roman Catholic Church today and all the Orthodox Churches world wide are discussed. The basic differences between the Orthodox Church and the Roman Catholic Church, as well as the Main-line Protestant Reformation Churches ar detailed.

Suggested reference books are listed in the back for those who would like to delve a little deeper into the history, spirituality and theology of the Orthodox Church. The first edition was published in 1988. While some minor additions and corrections were made in this second edition, by-and-large, the text follows the original.

Appreciation is expressed to my wife, Presbytera Sylvia Nicozisin and Father Paul Kaplanis, for their constructive criticism, meaningful contribution and pertinent suggestions. Thanks to my brother-in-law, George Souris, for proof-reading the manuscript in this edition and correcting spelling and grammatical errors. Finally, special thanks to my children, Georgeanne, Demetra and David for helping give the title to this book.

First Edition 1988 F.G.N.
Second Edition 1997

Dedicated to their Blessed Memories:

Demetrios and Stylianne Nicozisin

George and Helen Labros

Euphrosyne Maragedis

Byzantine Icon of Christ
By George Filippakis

Cover Design
By Euripides Kastaris

Table of Contents

PROLOGUE

In the Creed of Faith recited at each Baptism and Divine Liturgy we clearly state that we **"Believe in One, Holy, Catholic and Apostolic Church."** This Church in which we profess to believe was founded by the **Lord Jesus Christ!** It was established at a definite time in history. This Church has an evolution and a development. It has a history **—Church History!** Church History is the **Kingdom of God** here on earth and is divided into two parts:

Part One begins with the beginning of time —the creation of the world that we know and see.

Part Two begins with the **Birth of Jesus Christ** and continues until our present time.

It is important for us to know the **History of the Church** in order to make a better evaluation of Christ's teachings and His Mission of salvation to the world. Christ is more than a mere historical figure. He is the **Savior** Who wants all of us in His Kingdom. However, there is another reason we should study Church History. Jesus founded only One Church. But today we see many Christian Churches, each proclaiming to be the Church founded by Christ. Church history will help us evaluate our Holy Orthodox Church as the true historical Church. We will see that the Orthodox Church has not added false teachings nor substracted basic teachings but carried the same **Faith delivered to the Apostles** to this present day.

It is the contention and conviction of this author that the Orthodox Church has a tremendous contribution to make on the American Continent. But if Orthodox Christianity is truly to progress on the American Continent, She must have men, women and children deeply rooted in Her Tradition, thought and faith. It is hoped that this historical jet trip through Church History will help in some small way.

CHAPTER ONE

ANCIENT CIVILIZATIONS AND EMPIRES

The Church is made up of a body of believers in Jesus Christ, the Founder and Head of the Church. The mission of the Church is to save mankind for all eternity. Man was created to live in time and space. Therefore, mankind has a history. The Church, too, has a history because She lives and functions in time and space. But what was the world like before Jesus Christ came? How did civilizations develop? How did a particular Nation, Israel, become the Chosen People of God? Finally, how and why was Christ, the Messiah, born of this people?

ORIGIN OF CIVILIZATIONS

Civilization developed in the Tigris-Euphrates River Valley. It was known as the Mesopotamian Civilization (3500 B.C.) and corresponds to the one mentioned in the Old Testament. It extended to the Nile River, and from it emerged the Egyptian Civilization. Two other civilizations, the Indus River Valley in Northern India and the Yellow River Valley in China (both 3000-2000 B.C.), also emerged. While there were other civilizations too, these three are the most important in world history and are mentioned in the various books of the Old Testament in one form or another.

DEVELOPMENT OF EMPIRES

The Egyptians emerged as the ruling power sometime after 3000 B.C. and lasted for many centuries. Two of the many tribes they warred against, the Semites and Hittites, are mentioned in the Old Testament. Some of the Semites settled in Babylon, the Mesopotamian area; and from them sprung the Babylonian Civilization under Hammurabi (1947-1905 B.C.). The Hittites destroyed Babylon in 1750 B.C. They are important because they formed the links between the Ancient Near East and the primitive cultures of the Aegean and eastern Mediterranean Seas.

It was during this period of time that the Aramaeans, a Semitic people, developed along with the Hebrews and Phoenicians. The Aramaic language was adopted and remained until the time of Christ. The Hebrews (also called Israelites) were Semitic nomads who entered and settled in the Palestinian region some time around 2000 B.C.

The Exodus mentioned in the Bible took place probably around 1220 B.C. After the Israelites returned to Palestine, the history of this people passed several stages, the first of them being the Period of the Judges and Kings (Saul, David and Solomon) between 1100-975 B.C. After Solomon, Palestine was divided into kingdoms: the Kingdom of Israel, and the Kingdom of Judah. Both were conquered first by the Assyrians in 722 B.C. and later by the Babylonians in 586 B.C. The latter destroyed the Temple of Solomon and led thousands of Jews captive to Babylon.

The last five hundred years before Christ came witnessed the formation of three important empires which changed the world. The first was the **Persian Empire** (539-332 B.C.). During that time Emperor Cyrus permitted the Israelites to return to Palestine. The next empire, known as the **Hellenistic Empire,** began in 332 B.C. and lasted until 63 B.C. Alexander the Great defeated the Persians and conquered as far east as India. The third empire was the **Roman Empire.** The latter two periods are the most important because of their role in the acceptance and immediate spread of Christianity.

CHAPTER TWO

THE CHOSEN PEOPLE OF GOD

A NATION THAT BELIEVED IN ONE GOD

Looking back thousands of years, we see that there were many tribes and nations, each with its own religious beliefs and its own peculiar way of worshipping. Some worshipped animals, some stones, some the stars and some imaginary gods.

Among these nations there was a small nation in the Near East called Israel, whose people worshipped One God. The history of this nation is recorded in the pages of the Old Testament. Although these people believed in One God, from time to time they were tempted by their neighbors to embrace pagan religions. The Israelites' religion was a strict one and demanded much from them. But God intended that through this Nation all mankind would be brought back to His Kingdom, from which mankind had fallen.

God guided this Nation through lawgivers, priests, judges, kings, prophets and teachers. God promised mankind that He would send a Savior, the **"Messiah"** (the "Anointed One"). However, this Messiah would not establish an earthly kingdom as David and Solomon did, but a heavenly one, as was intended by God from the very beginning of time. This Nation was soon called the **"Chosen People"** or the **"Israelites."** The Israelites' religion was called **Judaism.**

GOD MAKES A COVENANT WITH ADAM

God created Adam and Eve because He wanted to share His love with others. When God created Adam and Eve,He gave them all the faculties and abilities to become perfect. To gain love Adam and Eve first had to learn **how** to love. To exercise authority they first had to learn to obey and find freedom through discipline. In order to accomplish these things God gave them the greatest gift:

He gave them **free will** to discern and decide for themselves what is **right** and what is **wrong.**

Adam and Eve were to take their **free will** and develop godliness, which in turn would assure them eternal fellowship with God. God did not make Adam and Eve **perfect in the absolute sense.** He made them **perfect in the potential sense.** God endowed them with the faculties and capability of becoming godly and godlike. This state of godliness is called **"theosis."** Once Adam and Eve achieved **theosis** they would inherit eternal life and live with God in perfect peace, harmony and happiness forever. This was the **Covenant Promise** that God made with Adam and Eve. The Bible says that God placed Adam and Eve in the Garden of Eden and instructed them to partake of all the fruits of the earth except the fruit from the tree of knowledge of good and evil. The Garden of Eden is a biblical metaphor which describes the godly and wholesome environment in which God placed the first man and woman. The tree of knowledge of good and evil is also a biblical metaphor which signifies the consequences of going against God, disobeying Him. The Garden of Eden consisted of all God's blessings which would facilitate the **theosis** growth. Conversely, partaking of the tree of knowledge would constitute the action of going against the **theosis** growth. But the choice had to be theirs!

Adam and Eve used their **gifts of free will** to turn away from their own true end, from the destiny and and eternal life God had prepared for them. Rather than embrace the blessed goodness God offered them, they chose to reject it. They sinned against God's Commandment and broke the **Covenant Promise** agreement with Him. This came to be known as the **Original Sin.** But God is not a God Who sits idly by and lets His people go unattended. As we shall see, God will offer His **Covenant Promise** again in different ways, as well as the means of eradicating the **Original Sin** in centuries to come. In the meantime, the offspring of Adam and Eve, and all the generations that follow, inherit the consequences of the broken **Covenant Promise** and the **Original Sin.**

GOD'S ORAL COVENANT PROMISE

Many years later, God found a good man called Abraham to whom He issued the **Covenant Promise** again. It is called the **Oral** or **Spoken Covenant Promise.** God instructed Abraham to leave his home and go to Canaan, where he would become the sole owner of all the land he could see. Abraham was told that his descendents would be as numerous as the stars in heaven. Abraham and his wife, Sarah, followed God's instructions and migrated to Canaan, where they gave birth to a son called Isaac.

Isaac had two sons, Jacob and Esau. Jacob conspired and connived with his mother, Rebeccah, to deceive his father, Isaac, in order to steal the birthrights from his brother Esau. When Esau discovered what had happened, Jacob fled for his life. During his flight Jacob repented for his sinful deeds and asked God's forgiveness. God forgave Jacob and renamed him **"Israel,"** which means **"Chosen One of God."** God promised Jacob/Israel and all his descendents that he would fulfill the **Covenant Promise** of eternal fellowship spoken orally to his grandfather, Abraham, and originally made with Adam and Eve.

The Israelites were greatly influenced by their neighbors, who were pagans and worshipped many gods. Instead of bringing their neighbors to God, as was their charge from God, the Israelites were led astray by them. As a result, the Israelites fell further away from God. But the Lord God had given His word that all nations on earth would be blessed through the **"Chosen People."** Therefore God kept reminding the Israelites of His **Covenant Promise** through special ambassadors, prophets and preachers. One of those special persons was Moses.

THE WRITTEN COVENANT PROMISE: THE TEN COMMANDMENTS

Jacob had many sons, one of whom was Joseph. Joseph was sold by his brothers into bondage and taken to Egypt where he was later cast into prison. Having interpreted the dreams of Pharaoh, the great Egyptian king, Joseph was made a princely ruler throughout all Egypt. A famine fell throughout the land and Jacob's descendents settled in Egypt, where they prospered. However, several generations later the Israelites fell out of Pharaoh's favor and were made slaves. God decided to return the Israelites to their own land. He instructed one of them, a man called Moses, to take them out of Pharaoh's land and return them to Canaan,the land given to Abraham. Moses obeyed. Along the way, Moses stopped and ascended Mount Sinai to receive instructions from God. It was here that God re-stated to Moses the same **Covenant Promise** He had made to Adam and Eve, and later renewed with Abraham and continued through Jacob. This was the **Written Covenant Promise** and is called the **Ten Commandments.** The Ten Commandments were placed in an Ark and constituted an ever-present reminder that God would fulfill His **Covenant Promise** if the Israelites kept theirs.

After the Israelites returned to their own land, God instructed them to form a Nation. But as time went by the Israelites fell deeper into sin and further away from God. God promised through His prophets that He would send a King to establish eternal fellowship between Himself and His people. This King would be the **Messiah.** The **Messiah** would come at **"the fullness of time,"** (Galatians 4:4), at the proper time, and fulfill once and for all the **Covenant Promise."** This **Messiah King,** as we shall see in the next chapter, is the **Lord Jesus Christ**, the Second Person of the Holy Trinity.

CHAPTER THREE

THE FULLNESS OF TIME

MAN'S NEED FOR A SAVIOR

When Adam and Eve drifted away from God, their fellowship with Him began to break down. Their relationship with Him became hazy and obscure. Their moral and ethical values deteriorated to the point that they could no longer discern right from wrong. They became afflicted with misery, guilt, sickness and disease. The greatest consequence was man's separation from God. Although civilization had come a long way and man's intellectual capacity had reached all-time of heights, his relationship with God had reached an all low. Sinfulness had become so pervasive that all humankind was on a collision course of self-destruction. But God could not permit this. Therefore, as St. Paul writes in his Letter to the Galatians, **"When the fulness of time was come, God sent forth His Son."** (4:4)

JESUS CHRIST AND THE BLOOD COVENANT PROMISE

God had given the Oral and Written Covenant Promise to the people of the Old Testament, but they did not keep it. This time God comes Himself in the Person of Jesus Christ about Whom the prophets had foretold. Christ came as **Prophet, High Priest and King:**

(a) As **Prophet,** Jesus Christ fulfilled what was foretold about Him in the Old Testament prophecies. He also gave firsthand knowledge about the Kingdom of God.

(b) As **High Priest,** Jesus Christ became both the Offerer and the Offered sacrifice. He offered Himself on the Cross for the life of the world.

(c) As **King,** Jesus Christ destroyed the power of death and hell and restored the Kingdom of Heaven. He also founded the Church as a means of bringing about the ruling power of God on earth.

Although their sins were forgiven, people still have the capacity to sin, to reject God and fall away from Him again. Therefore, Jesus Christ founded the Church as a vessel and channel through which there would be continuous flow of divine grace. This sanctifying grace flows through the sacramental and liturgical life of the Church.

CHRIST RESTORES THE KINGDOM

HE INSTITUTES THE CHURCH

During the three and one-half years Jesus taught, He gathered His disciples and followers and brought them to the knowledge of the Kingdom of God. He showed them His divinity in many ways. The greatest proof of His divine power was His Resurrection. He came back to life on Easter Pascha Sunday and reunited His followers. The Lord commanded His disciples to **"Go therefore and make disciples of all nations, baptizing them in the Name of the Father and of the Son and of the Holy Spirit, teaching them to observe all that I have commanded you: and lo I am with you always, to the end of the world."** (Matthew 28:19-20). Now the believers in Christ would be the **"Chosen People of God"** with Jesus Himself as their Lord.

CHRIST IS REJECTED BY THE ISRAELITES

The Israelites had waited in eager anticipation for a Messiah who would restore to them a royal kingdom like that of David and Solomon. Instead, the Messiah's Kingdom was the fulfillment of the Covenant Promise made by God. When the Israelites realized this, they became disenchanted with Christ. They completely rejected Him and asked Pontius Pilate, the Provincial Governor of Palestine, to give the death penalty. In doing this, the Israelites broke for the final time their

Covenant with God. They were no longer to be considered the **"Chosen Nation and People of God."** St. Paul said the Israelites' branch, which was deeply rooted in the tree of salvation, was cut off and a new branch was grafted on in its place. The new branch is the **"New Israel,"** which is the **Christian Church founded by Jesus Christ.** However, it is the same Covenant Promise made by God with Adam and Eve, restated to Abraham and Jacob, repeated through the Ten Commandments given to Moses, the same promise of eternal life and fellowship with God.

THE CHRISTIAN CHURCH IS ESTABLISHED

Forty days after the Resurrection Jesus assembled the nucleus of His Church, the eleven disciples, at the Mount of Olives near Bethany. He commanded them to remain in Jerusalem until the Holy Spirit would descend upon them and empower them to carry out His great commission: **"Go forth and preach to all Nations, baptizing them in the Name of the Father and the Son and the Holy Spirit."** Then Jesus ascended into Heaven. Ten days later, Pentecost Sunday, the Holy Spirit came upon them and the Christian Church was established. St. Peter preached the first Christian sermon and three thousand were baptized.

At first the Apostles restricted their preaching to Palestine. But within a short period of time Christianity began to spread over the entire civilized world. The early Christians gathered in private homes and reenacted the Last Supper with psalm-readings, prayers, sermons and by receiving Holy Communion.

During the first years the Christians used the Old Testament writings and exchanged letters or epistles. The New Testament did not exist as we know it today. Almost one hundred years went by before all the books of the New Testament were completed. They were fully validated by the Church at the First Ecumenical Council in 325 A.D.

CHAPTER FOUR

CHRISTIANITY SPREADS TO THE JEWS

JUDAISM

Judaism is a combination of culture and religion. Its most important points are: belief in One God, a set of moral and civil laws, certain ceremonies and customs, and a sacred literature. All these revolve around the people of Israel. It was from Judaism that Christianity first sprang, since God chose to have His Son born of the Jews. In fact, in the beginning, Christianity appeared to be just another part of Judaism, retaining many of the customs and rituals with a Christian interpretation.

PALESTINIAN JUDAISM

While there were many sects of Judaism at the time of Christ and the Early Christian Church, the four most prominent were the following:

> **The Scribes** were the professional teachers and scholars. It was their duty to interpret Scripture and Jewish literature and law. They held fast to the letter of the law and had a great influence over Palestinian Judaism. Jesus was constantly admonishing the Scribes for their distorted interpretations and misuse of Scripture.
>
> **The Sadducees** were another powerful group. They were the noblemen in political life who controlled the Temple in Jerusalem. They refused to make changes in their thinking or their duties, and they held to a strict understanding of the written Jewish law. They rejected resurrection, judgment after death, angels and the devil. The Sadducees fought the Christians relentlessly because they could not accept their basic doctrine in the Resurrection of Jesus Christ.

The Pharisees were by far the most difficult group for the Christians to cope with. They wanted the inherited faith pure from what they considered contamination. They, too, stood for the strict observance of the law. But unlike the Sadducees, they did believe in a life after death with rewards and punishment. According to scripture, the Pharisees instigated Jesus' betrayal, trial and death. They also participated in the stoning of St. Stephen the First Martyr and the persecution of the First Christians. Saul was a member of this group before he became Paul the Apostle to the Nations.

Hellenistic Jews were generally outside of Palestine. The Jews were scattered all over the Mediterranean world and were constantly exposed to Greek influence and thought. The Old Testament was translated into Greek because the Jews in Egypt were beginning to lose their faith and traditions, along with their language. This translation is known as the **Septuagint.** This mixture of Jewish traditions and Greek interpretation came to be known as Hellenistic Judaism. Christianity found Hellenistic Judaism a ready vehicle through which to spread the salvation gospel message of Jesus Christ. It was to these Jews that the Apostles first addressed themselves and made the inroads they did.

JUDAISM REJECTS CHRISTIANITY

Although Christianity sprang from Judaism, it was Christianity and not Judaism that had the greatest influence on mankind. Once the break with Judaism was finalized, there was no turning back. The Christian leaders used the network of roadways and the united Roman Empire to travel freely from one place to another. And wherever they went, they left an imprint of Jesus: love and faith. Once again, God had turned a tragedy into a hidden blessing. They were forced to flee; and, in so doing, they set into motion a religion that would leave an everlasting impression on the world.

CHAPTER FIVE

THE EARLY CHRISTIAN CHURCH

ST. PAUL, THE APOSTLE TO THE NATIONS

Paul, first called Saul, is one of the most dynamic personalities in the Early Christian Church. Paul's Jewish nationality and rabbinical training, his Greek classical education and his Roman citizenship provided him with a background that proved helpful in his missionary work. Sometime after his thirtieth year, a dramatic change took place in his life. In the Book of Acts, 9:3-9, we read that while on the road to Damascus to overtake Christian leaders and persecute them, he encountered Christ in a vision and was converted. After a period of introspection and preparation, Paul joined Barnabas as his companion and assistant. Paul soon assumed the leadership and went on Four Missionary Journeys from 45 A.D. through 64 A.D., where while in Rome he died a martyr's death.

THE APOSTOLIC SYNOD IN JERUSALEM (Acts 15:1-29)

After the First Missionary Journey, Paul and Barnabas returned to Jerusalem and met with the other Apostles and Christian leaders. They reported that they had christianized many Gentiles. But some of the Jewish Christian leaders insisted that the Gentile converts observe the Jewish Law and dietary requirements. Paul maintained that they should not be obligated to maintain Jewish religious ceremonies that were meaningless to them. A special meeting was called in Jerusaalem.

The Conference at Jerusalem, which was called the "Apostolic Synod," took place about 50 A.D. James, the Bishop of Jerusalem and Brother of the Lord, presided. Paul and Barnabas were successful in convincing the others that the Gentile Christians should not have to keep the Jewish Law. The Apostolic Synod made its decision known through letters to all the Christian Churches. This Synod was significant for two reasons: First, the

Christian Church thus became a Universal Church and her mission no longer was restricted to the Jewish people. Second, the Apostolic Synod set the precedent for Church leaders to come together in counciliar action in future internal and external conflicts.

THE FIRST CHRISTIAN WORSHIP

In the beginning, the Christians worshipped in the Synagogues. They also had evening worship services, which were called the **"Love Feasts"** or **"Holy Eucharist."** The Holy Eucharist was carried over from the Last Supper at which Christ commanded, **"Do this in remembrance of me."** After the Jewish leaders prohibited the Christians from entering the Synogogues, all worship was conducted in private homes. After a period of time, the Eucharist was performed in the morning hours on the Lord's Day (**"Kyriake"**). Although it differs slightly in appearance, the Eucharist is the **Divine Liturgy** we perform in all our Orthodox Churches on Sundays and Holy Days.

The First Christians did not have elaborately constructed Church buildings. They used whatever facilities could be found. During the period of persecution against the Christians, worship services were held in catacombs, cemeteries, basements, isolated and wooded areas, and any other available inconspicuous spot.

The Divine Liturgy was a dramatic re-enactment of the Life of Christ, beginning with the Nativity, the Public Ministry, the Last Supper, the Crucifixion and concluded with Holy Communion. It began with psalms, hymns and readings from the Old Testament. Books of the New Testament had not yet been written, but the miracles and teachings of Christ were related in the form of sermons. The clergyman of highest rank and seniority amongst those present would recite Jesus' words of institution, **"Take, eat, this is my body. Drink of it, all of you; for this is my blood of the New Testament, which is poured out for the forgiveness of sins."** (Matthew 26:26-28) He would then invoke the Holy Spirit to change the offered bread and wine into the very Body and very Blood of Jesus Christ, and all the baptized Christians would receive Holy Communion.

Justin Martyr, a second century A.D. philosopher saint describes the Divine Liturgy of his time this way:

> *"On the day of the Sun [Sunday] all who live in towns or in the country gather together to one place, and the letters of the Apostles or the writings of the prophets are read as long as time permits. Then when the reader has ceased, the presbyter verbally instructs and exhorts to the imitation of the good examples cited. Then all rise together, and prayers are offered. At length, as we have already described, prayer being ended, bread and wine and water are brought, and the presbyter offers prayer and thanksgiving, to the best of his ability, and the people assist by saying, 'Amen.' The Eucharistic elements are distributed and consumed by those present and to those who are not present it is sent by the ministry of the deacons."* (The First Apology, Chapter 67, Fathers of the Church Edition, Christian Heritage, Inc., New York.)

Another very ancient document, which was written at the beginning of the second century A.D., called "Didache [Teachings] of the Apostles," also says:

> *"As to the Eucharist, we give thanks in this way. First for the chalice: 'We thank Thee, our Father, for the Holy Vine of David, Thy servant, which Thou hast made known to us by Jesus Thy Servant. Glory to Thee for evermore!' For the bread: 'We thank Thee, our Father, for the life and the knowledge which Thou hast made known to us by Jesus Thy Servant. Glory to Thee for evermore! As the elements of this bread, scattered on the mountains, were brought together into a single whole, may Thy Church in like manner be gathered from other ends*

of the earth in Thy Kingdom; for Thine is the glory and the power, through Jesus Christ for evermore'." ("The Didache," Chapter 9, Early Christian Fathers, Library of Christian Classics. The Westminster Press, Philadelphia.)

HOLY SCRIPTURE

At the time of Jesus, the Old Testament was the only Scripture in existence. This is what Jesus interpreted and taught in the synagogues and on the Palestinian hillsides. To this Scripture the Apostles added the Oral Scripture, the Evangelion gospel message of Jesus Christ. It was not the mission of the Apostles and their immediate helpers to write. Oral teaching was the norm. It was due to special circumstances that the New Testament literature came into being. From 33 A.D. until than 50 A.D., everything was taught and passed on by word of mouth. What was passed on by word of mouth came to be the formal and official Evangelion gospel of Jesus Christ and was given authority by the leaders of the Church. It was between 50 and 100 A.D. that the books of the New Testament came into being as we know them today.

The first books written were letters of St. Paul to the Christian Churches of Thessalonika, Corinth, Ephesus, Philippi and areas of Asia Minor. He also wrote pastoral letters to Timothy, Titus and Philemon. St. Paul wrote to respond to certain problems and to clarify contemporary issues.

The gospels came to us in another way. Jesus taught the Apostles and the multitide orally. After Pentecost, the Apostles and their helpers also taught orally the teachings of Christ. They became the Church which both embodied the teachings of Christ and expressed them through preaching and living them. By the year 70 A.D., Mark, the first Evangelist to pull the collections together, found it necessary to prepare the Christians of Jerusalem for impending persecutions. St. Mark grouped the utterances of Jesus, the miracles, as well as the historical events of

Christ's life. This came to be the Gospel According to St. Mark. Sts. Matthew and Luke used Mark as a source and a guideline, but added collections which were both known and important to them and their local churches.

Unlike Matthew, Mark and Luke, the Apostle John wrote his collection of Jesus's sayings close to the end of the first century A.D. John responded to internal and external problems facing the Church of Christ and therefore found it unnecessary to mention the early life of Christ, the parables and much the other three included. All the teachings, sayings and unwritten scripture we call Holy Tradition.

THE NEW TESTAMENT CANON

By the middle of the second century A.D., a great deal of writing about Jesus Christ had been done. Some of this literature was fanciful and unreliable. Therefore, the Church, seeking to preserve the evanghelion gospel of Jesus Christ, found it necessary to distinguish clearly between those writings which did and those which did not possess Apostolic authority. This is what came to be known as the New Testament Canon. They employed three criteria:

> **Apostolicity.** It must have been taught by the Apostles who received it from Christ.
>
> **Catholicity.** It must have been mutually taught by all the Bishops, accepted and lived by all the Christians throughout the entire Church.
>
> **Conformity.** It must have not come into conflict nor contradiction with other scripture and teachings of the Church.

CHAPTER SIX

REVIEW OF THE FIRST THREE CENTURIES

The Early Christian Church spent most of the first three centuries of her existence being persecuted. The Christians were in a difficult position. They were no longer Jews, no longer Gentiles and no longer pagans. In the beginning, the Roman Government regarded them as an off-shoot Jewish sect. Since the Roman Emperor was considered to be divine, it was expected that all people of the nations under the Roman imperial throne express a form of worship to him. When the Christians did not comply, they were accused of being a threat to the State. Eventually, a full scale persecution set in which began about 64 A.D. and lasted some 250 years.

In spite of all the obstacles and persecutions, the Christian Church grew and expanded. Alexander the Great provided Hellenistic philosophy, literature and the classics, as well as the Greek language as vehicles. The Roman Empire provided the vast network of roads and communications for means of travel and expansion. Even the persecutions played an important part in divine destiny because they forced the Christians to scatter and take with them their zeal and missionary spirit. Wherever they went the new believers Christianized their neighbors. They preached and lived their faith.

During the first three centuries Christianity spread throughout Palestine, the eastern end of the Mediterranean Sea, the islands and the mainland of Asia Minor, Egypt, Greece and the Balkans. Westward, it spread to Rome, Britain, Gaul (France), Spain and Southern Europe. It was during these 250 years that the Church grew from infancy to maturity and began to take an active part and play a major role in world history. The years of persecution ended with the Edict of Milan in 313 A.D., after which the Church was permitted to worship openly and freely.

Jesus Christ brought a message of salvation to a troubled

world. He laid the foundation for achieving salvation by instituting the Church. The Church fought courageously and gallantly to ultimately win the freedom of expression heretofore allowed other religions. The Empire finally laid down its bloody sword and accepted the Nazarene's Church as a way of life. More than this, the Christian Church was destined to become the official religion of the Empire. But before this next phase can be studied, we must stop for a moment and see how the structure of the Christian Church developed and grew.

THE PENTARCHY

Pentarchy literally means **"Five Heads"** or leaders. The Patriarchal Sees of Rome, Alexandria, Antioch and Jerusalem emerged as the leading centers of the Christian Church. Constantinople was added as the fifth in the early fourth century. To understand this, let us look at the beginning of our Nation. In the beginning there were the cities of Jamestown, Plymouth Rock and Provincetown, but these were soon succeeded by cities like Boston, New York, Baltimore, Charleston, Savannah and Philadelphia. While the smaller cities were the original landings of the settlers, with the passing of time the larger cities emerged as the leading and prominent ones. Leading cities like Boston, Philadelphia and New York predominated in the American Revolution. It was to these cities that all the others looked for leadership. And even though Boston set the spark for the American Revolution, it was Philadelphia that heralded in the American Constitution. While New York became the first capital, it was succeeded by Washington, D.C.

In the Christian setting, Jerusalem was the seat of Christianity. In the early Apostolic times, St. Peter was the leader of the Christian Church in Jerusalem. The other Churches looked for guidance and direction from the Church of Jerusalem and Peter. Once Peter left Jerusalem and went to Antioch, both he and Jerusalem relinquished that primacy. James was elected the First

Bishop of Jerusalem. By the end of the third century, Rome assumed a position of honor and respect because it was the citadel of the Roman Empire. As we shall see in the next chapter, Constantine the Great will move the capital from Rome to Constantinople, where it will become an equally prominent center of Christendom. (Similar to the succession of prominence beween New York City and Washington,D.C.)

As the Church grew after Pentecost the Apostles selected men to assist them and then to succeed them. They were called Bishops. They, in turn, ordained priests to represent them in the local parishes and deacons to assist the bishops and the priests. Four types of Bishops emerged: **Rural Bishops, Metropolitan Bishops, Archbishops and Patriarchs.** Rural Bishops were in charge of medium-sized cities and the immediate region that surrounded them. Metropolitan Bishops were in charge of large cities and their surrounding areas. Archbishops were in charge of provincial counties and states. The Patriarchs were five; and they were in charge of the cities of **Rome, Constantinople, Alexandria, Antioch and Jerusalem,** forming the Pentarchy.

The **Pentarchy** was not a council that ruled the Church. Theirs was a position of honor and prestige. Although their opinions and judgments were revered and respected, they did not superimpose their authority upon any of their fellow Patriarchal Bishops, nor on the Archbishops, Metropolitan Bishops and Rural Bishops. To use an example today, neither the Metropolitan Bishop of New York City nor the Archbishop of the State of New York has the authority to infringe upon the authority and administration of the Churches of New Jersey, Rhode Island or Connecticut, even though they are smaller in size and population.

Occasionally Bishops of several provinces might meet in council to resolve certain problems. The highest ranking Bishop would preside but not impose authority. The decisions of that council were later ratified at the Ecumenical Councils. Problems concerning doctrines of the Church were discussed and resolved in general meetings of the bishops of all provinces. These general meetings are known as Ecumenical (Universal) Councils or Synods. Generally speaking, the Church developed a democratic form of administrative government right from Apostolic Times. As we shall see in subsequent chapters, that format changes in Western Europe. Eventually the Church in the West, which consisted of a Family of Independent Churches with their respective Independent Bishops, will be transformed into a Church with One Bishop, the Pope of Rome, as the Supreme Pontiff over the entire Church of Western Europe. This will be seen in later chapters.

BEGINNINGS OF THEOLOGY

As time went on, the mind of the Church was forged into a better method of stating what the Church believed and practiced. This is called theology. Theology is the study of God in Trinity, the evangelion gospel of salvation and eternal life, the principal purpose of the Church, and what Christians are required to believe.

In the beginning, it was sufficient to believe in the Lord Jesus Christ and to be baptized. But as time went on, Christians were challenged to defend and define what they held as Christian doctrines and truth. Those who followed the Apostles were called **Apostolic Fathers** and **Apologists.** The **Apostolic Fathers** wrote to define and clarify the teachings of Christ, the Bible and the Apostles. They represent the middle of the first century to the middle of the second century. The **Apologists** were prominent during the second and third centuries. They wrote in a systematic way to defend the Christain Faith by answering point by point the criticisms of their accusers. Theirs was an endeavor to enlighten the emperors and the populace during the persecutions.

CHRISTIAN WORSHIP

One of the greatest contributions made by Christian literature during this period was the legacy of the Divine Liturgy. The Divine Liturgy, which consisted of the Life of Christ in prayers, hymns, petitions, scripture and the consecration of the bread and wine into the Body and Blood of Jesus Christ, was expressed in all the facets of worship and life.

Sometime during the beginning of the third century, the class of catechumens came into existence. The catechumens were those being taught Christian doctrine and worship in preparation for baptism. They were permitted to participate in the first half of the Liturgy, Liturgy of the Word. This included the reading of scripture, sermon and special catechumen prayers. Then they were obliged to leave. The main part of the Liturgy was reserved for the baptized and practicing Christians. This is the setting when the second phase of Church History opened her doors. Constantine the Great saw the vision in the sky while crossing the Milvian Bridge and won his personal battle, and a victory for Christianity.

In the next three chapters we shall see the development and the contribution of the Byzantine Empire, the Ecumenical Councils, the Patristic Age, Christian literature, art, iconography and the formation of the Divine Liturgy. We shall also see the Rise of Islam and its threat to the Church.

CHAPTER SEVEN

THE BYZANTINE EMPIRE

AND THE ECUMENICAL COUNCILS

CONSTANTINE THE GREAT

The Roman Empire declined in the second and third centuries A.D., and by the beginning of the fourth century was divided into three sections. In 306 Constantine succeeded his father in the western part of the Empire. As he set out to reunite the Roman Empire, an event occurred which ultimately changed the whole picture of the Christian Church. As he was riding with his army toward the Milvian Bridge, near Rome, Constantine saw a cross of light in the sky with the inscription, **"In this sign conquer."** Constantine recaptured and reunited the Roman Empire. He issued the Edict of Milan in 313 A.D. which ceased the persecution of the Christian Church. He gave legal recognition and status to the Christian religion. He also moved the Capital of the Roman Empire to a city called **Byzantium** and thus led to the creation of the Christian Byzantine Empire. Nonetheless, the Byzantine Empire was the continuation of the Roman Empire but with headquarters located in the eastern part. Constantine was also instrumental in resolving doctrinal differences within the Christian Church by convening the First Ecumenical Council.

BEGINNING OF THE BYZANTINE EMPIRE

Byzantine History and Church History are so closely intertwined, they are practically inseparable. Constantine moved the capital of the Empire from the shores of the Tiber River in Italy to the city of Byzantium on the shores of the Bosphorus. The Empire took on the name Byzantine because the area was founded by Byzas, a Greek navigator in 657 B.C. The strategic and commercial seaport was at the far end of the Sea of Marmara between Europe and Asia Minor. Byzantium was later renamed Constantinople after Constantine the Great. It was also named **"New Rome"** because it replaced Rome as the capital of the Roman/Byzantine Empire. Christianity became the official religion of the Empire under Theodosios in 380 A.D.

THE FIRST ECUMENICAL COUNCIL 325 A.D.

At the beginning of the fourth century, two very crucial disagreements troubled the Church: The Arian controversy and the date to celebrate Easter. A quarrel arose between the Patriarch of Alexandria and one of his learned and eloquent priests. Arius taught that if Jesus was **born,** then there must have been a time when **He did not exist.** He **became** God. Therefore, there must have been a time when Jesus **was not God.** The First Ecumenical Council, convened by Constantine the Great in a city called Nicaea, proclaimed Arius' teaching as false. A young Deacon Athanasius from the Church of Alexandria helped find the proper language to explain that Jesus indeed had always been God. Athanasius, along with the Council Fathers, put into words what the Church had taught from the time of the Holy Apostles. What they wrote became the first seven articles of the **Creed** we recite at every Divine Liturgy and Baptism.

The problem of the Easter date was also resolved. Until that time some celebrated Easter with the Jewish Passover, others before, and others after the Jewish Passover. The First Ecumenical Council decreed that the Easter date each year must fall after the spring vernal equinox (equal daylight and nightime hours); after the first full moon after the spring vernal equinox; and, the Sunday after the Jewish Passover each year. Eastern Christians adhere to all three requirements whereas Roman Catholics and Protestants keep only the first two requirements. This is the reason why the two Easter dates are most often different.

THE SECOND ECUMENICAL COUNCIL 381 A.D.

This Council, convened in Constantinople, approved all the decisions of the First Council. It also condemned Macedonius who preached that the Holy Spirit was **inferior** to the Father and the Son in the Holy Trinity. The Council Fathers completed the **Creed** by adding five articles to the original seven. This Creed came to be known as the **Nicaea-Constantinoplitan Creed.** The Second Ecumenical Council also declared: **"The Bishop of Constantinople shall rank next to the Bishop of Rome, because Constantinople is the New Rome."**

THE THIRD ECUMENICAL COUNCIL

The Third Ecumenical Council was called into session in the city of Ephesus, Asia Minor, in 431 A.D. Nestorius, a Bishop of Constantinople, taught that the Holy Virgin Mary gave birth to Christ and therefore should be called **"Christotokos."** The Council proclaimed that the Lord Jesus Christ, the Son of God and complete Man, was conceived in the Virgin Mary and given birth to Him by her. Therefore, she is called **"Theotokos."** Even though Jesus Christ was complete God and complete Man, the union between His divine nature and his human nature took place in such a unique way that one did not disturb the other.

FOURTH ECUMENICAL COUNCIL

It seems that during this period of church history the Person of Jesus Christ was difficult to describe and understand in human terms. Once again, the two natures of Christ, divine and human became the cause of controversy. A group called **Monophysites** believed that at some point Jesus' divine nature consumed and eliminated His human nature. The word **"monophysite"** means **"one nature."** The Fourth Ecumenical Council was convened in a city called Chalcedon, in 451 A.D. This

Council condemned the monophysite teachings and declared that Jesus Christ had **two natures: divine and human, full and complete**, as defined in previous Councils. Unfortunately, a segment of the Church separated and continue to be separated until this day. They are the Armenian Church, the Coptic Church in Egypt and other parts of Northern Africa, as well as the Jacobite Church. Collectively they are called **Non-Chalcedonian Churches.**

FIFTH ECUMENICAL COUNCIL 553 A.D.

The fourth-century Arian controversy made its way into Western European Christianity in the sixth century. In the eastern part of the empire the Monophysite controversy continued to plague the Church. Following the established tradition of his predecessors, Justinian the Great called the Fifth Ecumenical Council in Constantinople which declared once and for all the teachings of the Church regarding the two Natures of the Lord Jesus Christ.

SIXTH ECUMENICAL COUNCIL 680 A.D.

The Monophysite controversy did not subside. Many attempts were made to settle this dangerous controversy. One such attempt said, "Yes, Jesus Christ did have two natures, divine and human, but the human nature was motivated and influenced by the divine nature." In other words, the divine nature made all the decisions and the human nature carried and acted them out. This teaching came to be known as **"Monothelitism," "one will"** or **"one initiative, "** which was divine. But the Sixth Ecumenical Council convened in Constantinople called **Monothelitism** a heresy and condemned it. The Council proclaimed: **"Christ has two natures with two activities: As God He worked miracles, rose from the dead and ascended into heaven. As Man He performed the ordinary acts of daily life. Each nature exercises its own free will."**

CHAPTER EIGHT

THE GOLDEN AGE OF THE CHURCH

The **Golden Age** was a period during which some of the most learned and profound theologians of the Christian Church lived and wrote. These theologians are called the **Church Fathers.** An Orthodox Matins hymn calls them, *"A divine army, God-inspired soldiers of the Camp of the Lord, most brilliant luminaries of the noetic firmament, impregnable towers of the mystical Zion, scented flowers of paradise, golden mouths of Christ, the boast and delight of the whole universe."* These Christians scholars used their wisdom, knowledge and devotion to weave the garment of sound faith for Christ's Church. It was during this **Golden Age**, the fourth through the ninth centuries, that the greatest Christian literature was compiled. The Church Fathers helped to mold a unique tradition, the **Byzantine**, which had a tremendous impact not only in the East, but in the West, as well.

THE PATRISTIC PERIOD

At the beginning of the fourth century, approximately 10% of the inhabitants of the Roman Empire were Christians; by the end of the same century, 60% were Christians. The Christian religion was still relatively young in the pagan world; therefore, teachers were needed to explain the faith. Also during the fourth and fifth centuries several theological controversies arose within the Church which needed to be resolved. These controversies were called **Christological** disputes, because as we saw in the last chapter, certain people were teaching false doctrines about Jesus Christ. By the time of the Fifth Ecumenical Council (553), the Church had developed a roster of Christian scholars and writers who were considered the undisputed bearers of **Orthodox Tradition.** After these sixth-century writers, there followed others in the seventh, eighth and ninth centuries.

The writings of these learned Church leaders outlined and defined the Christian Faith and laid the foundation of Orthodox Theology. These select theologians are referred to as the **Church Fathers,** or the **Patristic Fathers.** Therefore, the fourth through ninth centuries are appropriately called the Patristic Period.

MONASTICISM

Who were the Monks? How did Monasticism begin? Why were the Monasteries so important to the Church? During the persecutions Christians were forced to witness their faith in Jesus Christ. Once the Edict of Toleration became effective in 313, a new type of martyr appeared on the Church scene --the monk. He sacrificed and abandoned worldly riches and position to live a life as close to God as possible. These new martyrs left worldly cares in order to seek clearer vision of God and to attempt to learn the true meaning of life. Monasticism served as a guiding light and beacon to the rest of the Christian world. It began in the Egypt desert during the fourth century and very rapidly spread to Syria, Constantinople, Palestine and Italy.

Monasticism was a way of life. It meant withdrawal, either completely or partially, into a life of undisturbed prayer, worship and meditation. The monks were an ever-constant reminder to Christians that the Kingdom of God was not to be found in this world, but in Heaven. The early monks preached, heard confessions, counseled, copied manuscripts of scripture and spiritual writings, developed the art of iconography, opened monastic schools for theological training, and often gave their lives in defense of Orthodoxy.

CHRISTIAN LITERATURE AND ART

By the fourth century there were three principal areas in the East where Christian literature and art had developed abundantly; namely, Alexandria of Egypt, Antioch of Syria and Ephesus of Asia Minor. These centers found their source of inspiration in the classical tradition of Hellenistic culture. After Byzantium became the capital of the Empire, it slowly and gradually became the center of this culture. A unique style of Christian literature appeared on the scene during the fourth through sixth centuries. Hellenistic writings and art were infused with the forces of theology and piety, and from this union emerged Byzantine literature, hymnology and art.

As was indicated in the previous chapter, this new style of literature found its first expression in Patristics Writings. When the Church was able to come out of the catacombs and was permitted to worship freely without fear of persecution, the Divine Liturgy underwent its final revisions; and magnificent churches were constructed. Along with these came the development of Byzantine hymnology and art. These three elements —**literature, hymnology** and **art**— were united in a very unique way to convey a theological understanding of the Risen Christ in instruction, prayer and experiential worship.

Byzantine literature is divided into prose and poetry. Prose appears in many forms. Among those forms are the theological writings of the Church Fathers, historical writings, hagiography (lives of saints), letters, sermons, funeral orations and apologetic treatises.

BYZANTINE POETRY

Byzantine poetry is synonymous with Church hymns and prayers. The hymns of the first five centuries were derived from the style of ancient Greek music and were chanted on a monotone drone note, similar to the chorus of the ancient Greek theatre. This was also the style of Jewish chant in the synagogues during New Testament times. The sixth century marks the beginning of a new era in Church hymnography. A different style of hymns and chants was introduced by Romanus the Melodist (d. 560). It is said that Romanus wrote at least 1000 hymns, some 80 of which are still preserved. The subjects are sermons in poetic form and range widely from the Old Testament stories, such as Joseph's trials and tribulations, to New Testament episodes of Christ's Life. He also wrote festive hymns for Easter and Christmas.

BYZANTINE ICONOGRAPHY

Iconography has always been a part of the Orthodox conscience. It is an art that dates back to the persecution period when the walls of the catacombs were filled with drawings of Jesus as the Good Shepherd. With the peace of the Church in the early fourth century and as the Church became more theologically oriented, God, Jesus Christ and events of scripture began to be depicted in drawings and paintings. The Golden Age Period crystallized a style of art that came to be known as **Byzantine Iconography.** Byzantine iconography consisted of paintings, icons, frescoes and mosaics which reflected persons or scenes. Byzantine iconography is quite different from the style of paintings found in Europe and America. The latter are greatly influenced by Renaissance art which attempts to make the figures and faces earthly by using rich hues of blues, reds, oranges, etc. In contrast, Byzantine iconography does not intend to recreate an earthly-looking person, but one reflected in God's heavenly dimension. Secondly, the colors are soft and natural looking so as not to distract from the person or event portrayed.

In addition to Byzantine iconography, Byzantine art reflected itself in the sculpturing and carving of crosses, icons, chalices and a multitude of other sacred objects. The construction of magnificent church edifices also belongs to this category. The greatest architectural gem of the Golden Age was the construction of **Saint Sophia** in Constantinople by Justinian the Great in 537. Considering that steel beams and girders were unknown at the time, it is remarkable that the huge dome could be set so accurately upon the pillars and supporting walls. Saint Sophia is a Turkish museum today, but it continues to be a lasting monument of Byzantine art of the Golden Age.

THE DIVINE LITURGY

The greatest and most classic example of Christian literature during the Golden Age was the formation and final development of the Divine Liturgy. It was noted in a previous chapter that the Christians of Apostolic times continued going to the synagogues; but once they were banished from the synagogues, they worshipped the Eucharist in homes. With the onslaught of persecutions, they worshipped the Eucharist wherever they could. Nevertheless, the formation and structure of the Eucharist continued to develop so that by the Peace of the Church (313 A.D.) the Divine Liturgy had been fairly well established. The two authentic documents of Justin Martyr's First Apology (151) and St. Hippolytus' Apostolic Tradition (215) describe for us in detail the Liturgies of their times. The authority of these two writers is enhanced by the fact that both had traveled extensively in the West and the East. Although the Liturgy was established by the early fourth century it continued to develop and grow into different styles or rites, both in the East and the West.

EASTERN OR BYZANTINE LITURGIES

The Byzantine Liturgy combined the teachings, practices and the rites of Jerusalem, Antioch and Constantinople. There were many other liturgies in the East; but as Constantinople became the great city for Eastern Christendom during the Golden Age, the Byzantine Liturgy became the Eucharistic Service for the entire East. By the beginning of the sixth century the Byzantine Liturgy became fixed in four styles: **Liturgy of St. Basil, Liturgy of St. John Chrysostom, Liturgy of St. James, and the Liturgy of the Pre-Sanctified,** which is a Lenten Liturgy. The latter combines the first half of a Vesper Service and the second half of the Eucharist without the Consecration.

WESTERN LITURGIES

The Liturgies of Western Christendom did not become uniform as rapidly as in the East. There was no uniform, authoritatively-fixed Liturgy in the West until the sixteenth century Protestant Reformation. While the Eastern part of the Empire remained united, the Western part had a severe breakup. Territories in the West were invaded, conquered and occupied by barbaric tribes. Gothic Tribes occupied Spain and Italy, Gauls occupied France, and Anglo-Saxons occupied England. As Britain, France, Italy, North Africa and Spain became Tribal States, native liturgies evolved from the ancient Hippolytan Rite. In the northern part of Italy there was the Ambrosian/Milonese Rite; Spain had the Mozarabic Rite; Ireland and Scotland, the Altic Rite; France, the Gallican Rite; and Southern Italy, the Roman Rite. In later centuries Charlemagne imposed the Gallican Rite on the German, French, English and Spanish States. Later, the Gallican Rite was imposed upon Rome and thus replaced the ancient Roman Rite.

The Western Churches (Roman Catholic, Anglican and Main-Line Protestant Reformation Churches) followed the Gallicanized Roman Rite. This Rite was altered many times from the sixth through sixteenth centuries by innovations, additions, accretions and insertions. Since Vatican II Council (1965) the Roman Catholic Church has embarked on a liturgical renewal to restore the ancient Roman Rite. Protestant scholars are also involved in a liturgical renewal.

Roman Catholic and Protestant liturgical scholars are discovering that the Orthodox Church has kept the early form of corporate worship in the Divine Liturgy. The Orthodox Liturgy has made its way from Jerusalem, Antioch and Constantinople, to the Balkan Countries, the Slavic Nations, India, Japan, Korea, the Aleutian Islands, Africa, Western Europe and to America. The Orthodox Liturgy is relevant for all times and all places. What is needed is to have Orthodox Christians attend and participate more meaningfully in the Liturgy! This is a challenge for both long-standing Orthodox Christians and those who embrace the Faith!

CHAPTER NINE

RISE OF ISLAM AND ICONOCLASM

THE SEVENTH ECUMENICAL COUNCIL

Long before Christianity came to the world there were people of Semitic origin called Arabs, who occupied the Arabian peninsula. They lived in a territory that stretched east to the Persian Gulf, south to the Indian Ocean, west to the Red Sea, and north to the Syrian desert. Their religion was a primitive one that consisted of worshipping stones, trees, springs of water and the stars. Politically they were Nomadic Tribes that settled and formed little cities and hamlets along the trade routes and caravan roads leading from the south to the north, from Yemen to Palestine, and the Sinai peninsula.

The richest city along this route was Mecca, famous long before Muhammed's appearance. Second in importance was the city of Yathrib, later called Medina. There were many Jews among the merchants of Mecca and Yathrib. In addition there were Christians from the Byzantine Provinces of Palestine, Syria and Abyssinia who had penetrated the peninsula. Mecca became the central gathering point for mixed populations in the area. Mecca was an exceptional commercial center in the midst of an arid wilderness, and was frequented by merchants from all the Arabian tribes.

Under the influence of Judaism and Christianity the Arabs of Mecca became acquainted with the belief in One God. Even during the time of Justinian the Great there were large Arab tribes which had Monophysitic leanings. This is noteworthy, because it gives some insight into why the Monphysitic Syria, Palestine and Egypt were so easily conquered in the seventh and eighth centuries by the Arabs. By the sixth century the Arabs had accepted Monotheism (belief in One God) which they borrowed from Judaism and Christianity. But the man who was solely responsible for the unification of the Arab Tribes, who founded a world religion and became both prophet and chief of a political nation called **Islam**, was Muhammed.

MUHAMMED

Muhammed, born in 570 in Mecca, believed that he had received the gift of divine revelation, that God spoke to him through the Archangel Gabriel. These sayings were copied by his disciples and make up the **Koran**, the Islamic "Bible." Muhammed began as a preacher to inspire his people to submit to One God, Allah. The word **Islam** means submission, and **Muslim** means one who has submitted.

Muhammed was forced to leave Mecca because of his radical teachings and went to Yathrib, which was by this time called Medina. The year of his flight (622) is called *Hejira* and is the year 1 for the Islamic calendar. At Medina Muhammed won a large following. The first mosque, place of worship, was erected there. Muhammed began a series of holy wars on caravans, which later unleashed the desire for national conquest. He returned to Mecca in 630 and made it the religious center of Islam. Shortly after his death his religion spread all over Arabia.

ISLAMIC TEACHINGS

The religious teachings of Islam are very simple. The Islamic God is the God of Judaism and Christianity. The belief in One God is absolutely imperative for Islam. Muhammed did not reject the Old Testament Prophets. He regarded Jesus Christ not as divine but as next to the last in the line of prophets, which culminated in himself, the last and greatest messenger of Allah. Paradise awaited the faithful believers after death, especially those who died in battle against the infidels, the non-believers. Muslims were prohibited from eating pork and drinking wine, and they gave alms to the poor.

Islam has neither priests nor sacraments. There are, however, a number of ritual observances which are compulsory. Prayers at the mosques are recited by a leader and usually consist of passages taken from the

Koran. Prayer five times a day facing Mecca is a strict requirement. The five times of daily prayer are to help invoke God the rest of the twenty-three hours of the day. And if he can afford it, the Muslim is required to make a pilgrimage to Mecca at least once during his lifetime.

ISLAMIC CONQUESTS

A century afer Muhammed's death, the crescent banner of Islam waved over territory which stretched from the Pyrenees and Southern France to the Indus River. The fire of nationalism and religion that united them is astonishing. They found a faith that kindled them with a new kind of fanaticism. In Egypt, Syria and Palestine there were heretical Christian groups who were only too glad to exchange Byzantine masters for Muslim ones who promised them religious tolerance and lower taxes. The Arabs advanced into Mesopotamia in 637, and by 650 they completely erased the Persian Empire. Proceeding east to the Indus River, they captured most of India. Alexandria fell in 642 and Cairo became the capital.

The conquest of North Africa followed the Egyptian conquest. In 697 they took Carthage and all of North Africa, and in 711 they crossed the Straits of Gibraltar and attacked Spain. After overrunning Spain, they advanced across the Pyranees and got as far as Frankish Gaul. They were finally stopped in the West at Tours in 743 by the Frankish ruler Charles Martel. Spain was eventually recaptured by the Christians. Meanwhile in the eastern Mediterranean, Islamic marauders were constantly menacing Constantinople. Emperor Leo III defended the city and held them back. The Islamic armies retreated behind the Taurus Mountains, and thus Asia Minor remained a Byzantine province for several more centuries.

ISLAMIC CALIPHATES

Muhammed did not name a successor. At first, his close associates succeeded him and then a hereditary succession began. By the time Egypt, Syria, Palestine and Persia were captured, a new type of tribal government came into existence called **Caliphates.** The Caliphates sprang up like city-states in Damascus, Bagdad, Cairo and Tunisia. Since the Koran was written in Arabic, Muslims, whatever their nationality and background, learned enough Arabic to recite it. Thus, after a period of time, the Arabic tongue became the universal language for all Muslims.

Today Islam predominates in the Persian Gulf Area, the Middle East, Turkey and the North African coastline. It is also found in some Southeastern States of the Soviet Union, Central Africa, Western Europe and America.

ICONOCLASTIC PERIOD

The beginning of the eighth century found the Byzantine Empire in much danger from the Islamic onslaughts. The Church, too, faced another struggle which centered around the use of icons and was called the **Iconoclastic Period.**

The **Iconoclasts** were purists who were suspicious of any religious art which represented God, Jesus Christ, the Theotokos or the Saints in any artificial or material way. They demanded that the Church rid herself of every form of art that found expression in this way and that such religious art be destroyed or broken, as the word iconoclast implies. The **Iconodules,** on the other hand, were those who believed that icons served to preserve the doctrinal teachings of the Church. They were man's dynamic way of expressing the Divine through beauty and art.

FIRST PERIOD OF THE ICONOCLAST CONTROVERSY

The Iconoclast controversy lasted for over 100 years and fell into two phases or periods. The first began in 726, when Leo III the Isaurian instituted his program of reform. In 730 he issued a proclamation that all icons must be removed from the churches, monasteries and homes, and be destroyed. He even called a Council in 754 and forced his viewpoint on the delegates. His son, Constantine V enforced the decisions of his father with sword and fire. By 765 a savage persecution against the Iconodules was underway because they were regarded as rebels against God and the Emperor. This was the time when monasticism had the responsibility of defending the faith. Many monks became the "new Martyrs." It was also a grave period of time when much art and iconography were removed and destroyed, forever lost to our era. Constantine V died in 775 and was succeeded by his son Leo IV who, although held Iconoclastic views, at least put a stop to the persecution of monks. When he died, his widow the Empress Irene suspended all persecutions.

SEVENTH ECUMENICAL COUNCIL

In 787 the Seventh Ecumenical Council was called in Nicaea which upheld the position of the Iconodules. The Council said:

> ***"We define that the holy icons, whether in color, mosaic, or some other material, should be exposed in the holy Churches of God, on the sacred vessels and liturgical vestments, on the walls, furnishings, and in houses and along the roads, namely, the icons of our Lord God and Savior Jesus Christ, that of our Lady the Theotokos, those of the venerable angels and those of all holy men. Whenever these representations are contemplated, they will cause those who look at them to commemorate and love their prototype. We define also that they should be kissed and that they are an object of veneration and honor (timitiki proskynisis), but not of real worship (latreia), which is reserved for Him Who is the Subject of our faith and is proper for the Divine Nature alone...The honor rendered to this icon is in effect transmitted to the prototype; he who venerates the icon, venerates in it the reality for which it stands."***

Father John Meyendorff writes: ***"The Orthodox Church regards the veneration of icons as something dogmatically wholesome and sound. This is ultimately because of the reality of the Incarnation of the Word."*** (The Orthodox Church)

ST. JOHN OF DAMASCUS

The staunchest champion of the icons in the first period was John of Damascus (675-745). John came from a distinguished Christian family in Damascus. Since Syria was under one of the Muslim Caliphates, his schooling was supervised by the Caliphate Court. An outstanding student, he excelled in political science and embarked on a political career which brought him to a position comparable to that of Prime Minister. All during his career he remained a devout Orthodox Christian. He often preached sermons and participated in the Iconoclastic controversy. He wrote three famous and convincing letters explaining the deep doctrinal meaning of the icons. His writings reached Constantinople, where they were read in defense against the Iconoclast leaders. Someone sent copies to the Caliph of Damascus, who, upon reading them became suspicious that John would betray the city to the Byzantine Emperor. The Caliph called John before him and after a debate, he became enraged and had John's hand cut off with a sword so that he could never write again. In answer to prayer, John's hand was miraculously healed. The Caliph was sorry and tried to restore him to his high position. But John was so moved with the miracle that he entered the Monastery of St. Sabbas in the desert of southern Palestine. It was there that John spent many years writing religious poems and hymns.

St. John's magnificent contribution to Byzantine music, poetry and hymnography are unparalleled in history. However, his most outstanding work is a writing called ***"An Exact Exposition of The Orthodox Faith."*** In this classic treatise St. John of Damascus drew from all the Church Fathers of the Patristic Period and wrote a systematic theological summary of all the basic doctrines of the first seven centuries. This monumental and valuable work has been the foundation for Orthodox theology. It was also used extensively by St. Thomas Aquinas, the thirteenth century Father of Western Scholasticism, and remains a classic theological document for all Christian denominations until today. St. John of Damascus also wrote many other theological treatises. As stated earlier, he also wrote beautiful and meaningful hymns, some of which are found in the Orthodox Funeral Service.

THE ICONOCLASTIC CONTROVERSY IS RESOLVED

Leo V came to the throne in 813, and in 815 he began again the persecutions against the Iconodules. Leo's son Theophilus increased the persecutions with strict and stern laws. The reign of terror ended when Theophilus' widow, Empress Theodora, brought to a halt the persecutions once and for all in 843. The final victory of the holy icons in 843 is known as **"The Triumph of Orthodoxy."** The monks and the clergy came in procession and restored the icons in their rightful places on the First Sunday of Lent that year. Since that time Eastern Christendom commemorates the triumphant event with a special service on the First Sunday of Lent, **"The Sunday of Orthodoxy."**

The Iconoclast Controversy had at least one important result: It opened the door to a second Golden Age in Byzantine Art —the ninth through the fifteenth centuries.

CHAPTER TEN

BYZANTIUM'S CONTRIBUTION TO CIVILIZATION AND THE CHURCH

One cannot study Church History, or any history for that matter, without studying the Byzantine Empire. Byzantine History continues to live in the Orthodox Church. Just as modern Roman Catholicism crystallized in the Middle Ages, so did Orthodoxy acquire its present form throughout the formative years of the Byzantine Empire. Worship, iconography and our whole patristic heritage were given their shape and style in Byzantium. The Byzantine Period must be recognized as an integral part in the history of the **"One, Holy, Catholic and Apostolic Church."** All the modern Orthodox Churches throughout the world, from the viewpoint of history, are the Church of Byzantium. What was Byzantium's contribution to Civilization and the Church? This is the question that this chapter will consider.

BYZANTIUM IS IGNORED

It is most unfortunate that the history textbooks of both Europe and the United States are primarily and exclusively based on Edward Gibbon's "The Decline and Fall of the Roman Empire" (1776-1788). Although the four volumes are a masterpiece of literature and a landmark in the history of historical research, very little emphasis is given to the contribution of Byzantine Civilization to the Church and to the world. Marcus Ward, a historical scholar from South India writes: *"Gibbon has done much to give currency to the idea that the Byzantine story is merely the last unhappy chapter of Roman history."* (*"The Byzantine Church,"* Christian literature Society, Madras, India, 1953. p.viii.)

Ward says that A.L. Rowse in his book, *"The Use of History,"* declares him [Gibbon] to be *"very unjust to the*

Byzantine Empire, which represents a remarkable positive achievement that Gibbon seems to have been unaware of. For a thousand years Byzantium stood guard at the gate of the European civilizations against the Turks, and even then would never have fallen if it had not been irretrievably weakened by the disgraceful onslaught of the West in the Latin Crusade (1204)." (Ibid. p. viii.)

BYZANTIUM FORMS AN UNBROKEN CHAIN

It has been noted that Byzantium served for over one thousand years as the bulwark of Christendom against the invading Islamic hordes. She was more than a passive defense line. First, she preserved the heritage and legacy of Hellenism; and second, she developed a culture all her own. This Byzantine culture was a remarkable amalgamation of the philosophy and literature of Ancient Greece with the doctrinal teachings of Christianity. Constantinople became a cultural center for the classics of Byzantium and, consequently, had significant influence upon the development of Western Civilization.

The Roman Empire, emerging after the decline of ancient Greece, originally encompassed East and West. Both parts of the Empire possessed the cultural and religious legacies which belonged to the early centuries of Christianity. Once the capital was transferred to the shores of the Bosphorus, the West dropped the language of the Greeks and adopted the Latin language. In addition, the western part of Christendom began to absorb the customs, habits and practices of each successive tribe of invading barbarians. Conversely, the East kept the Greek element of the Hellenistic Period, perpetuated it, built upon it and preserved it until the Fall of the Byzantine Empire in 1453. But it did not stop there; it continues unbroken today in the Church of Orthodoxy all over the world.

The secret of Byzantine political and military strength lay largely in its continued economic prosperity. Constantinople became the repository for merchandise from all over the known world. Its fabulous wealth astonished travelers from western and northern Europe. Merchant routes were established with India and the Far East. The Byzantines brought silk worm eggs from China, which eventually made possible a thriving native silk industry throughout all of Asia Minor and the Near East.

The heart and center of the Byzantine imperial system was Constantinope. To make this city the ***"New Rome,"*** worthy of its dignity as the capital and successor of the ***"Old Rome,"*** Constantine the Great and his successors spared no expense. The city was admirably and securely fortified. Gilded domes, marble steps and magnificent mosaic decorations, so abundant in the Churches, palaces and public buildings, made the city a show piece of the East.

The citizens of the Byzantine Empire were profoundly interested in matters of religion. Not only did the Emperors take an active part in Church affairs, but the average citizen was absorbed in the general theological controversies. As we have seen repeatedly, Byzantium set the stage for the Seven Ecumenical Councils out of which were forged the pillars of the Christian Faith.

BYZANTIUM'S CONTRIBUTION TO WESTERN CIVILIZATION

The world's debt to Byzantium is immense! In the spheres of learning, politics, economics, law and art, it is difficult to determine what amount of originality can be claimed for the foundation of Western Civilization as we know it. In the sixth century, under Justinian the Great, Byzantium recaptured much of Italy and established the so-called Exarchate of Ravenna, which placed Rome and a good part of Italy under the Byzantine Empire. The Exarchate remained under Byzantium until 751, when Ravenna was finally captured by the Lombards. Before its collapse, however, Ravenna became a center of Byzantine cultural influence, especially in art. To this day in Ravenna there are magnificent Byzantine churches of priceless historical value.

During the eighth and ninth centuries, according to some Byzantine scholars [for example, Dr. Deno Geanakoplos, Yale], as many as 50,000 eastern monks fled to Calabria and other parts of southern Italy to escape the persecutions of the Byzantine Iconoclastic Emperors. By the eleventh century many parts of Southern Italy became *Byzantinized* in both culture and religion. These hamlets of Orthodox scholars in the West laid the seeds and footings for the Western Renaissance Period of the fourteenth and fifteenth centuries. Recall that El Greco was born Domenikos Theotokopoulos in 1541 in Crete and trained as an icon painter in the Byzantine tradition. From Crete he went to Venice and Rome, and finally to Toledo, Spain, where until his death in 1614, his work bore the evidence of his Byzantine heritage. But Byzantium also made a monumental contribution to the Slavic Nations of the north. As we shall see in the next chapter, both Byzantium and the Eastern Orthodox Church will permeate in the Slavic north to form the Bulgarian Orthodox, Serbian Orthodox, Ukranian Orthodox, Rumanian Orthodox, Albanian Orthodox and Russian Orthodox Churches. From these, as well as the ancient Patriarchal Churches of Jerusalem, Antioch, Alexandria and Constantinople, stem all Orthodox Churches around the world. It is of paramount important that the student of Church History know these facts.

CHAPTER ELEVEN

CHRISTIANITY SPREADS TO THE SLAVIC NATIONS

The Slavs were the marauding barbarians of Eastern Europe. It is generally accepted that they existed as an ethnic group as early as the seventh century B.C. But nobody really knows the exact region in which they began to develop. The early Slavic tribes are divided into three groups:

The Western Slavs who migrated to the Elbe and the areas toward the Baltic Sea. They were called the Moravians, and they were the ancestors of the Poles, the Czechs and the Slovaks. They came under the influence of Western Europe, adopted the Latin language and eventually became Roman Catholics.

The Southern Slavs who pushed across the Carpathian Mountains into the Balkan peninsula south of the Danube River. They were the ancestors of the Serbians, the Croatians, the Dalmatians and the Bulgarians. The Croatians and the Dalmatians later united with the Hungarian Empire and passed over to the jurisdiction of the See of Rome. Part of the remaining groups settled in the area just north of Thessalonika and became the Serbian Nation, which remained with the Eastern Orthodox Church. The other part, which settled around the Black Sea, mingled with the remnant of the Hunnic Nation and became the Bulgaria State. They, too, remained with the Eastern Orthodox Church.

The Eastern Slavs who made their way eastward toward the Dnieper River, the Steppes, the Caucasus and the Volga River. This is called the Russian plain and extended from eastern Europe to central Siberia, from the Artic Ocean southward to the Carpathian Mountains, the Black Sea, the Caspian Sea and Central Asia. They also remained Eastern Orthodox.

STS. CYRIL AND METHODIUS

Among the Slavic tribes were the Moravians,who settled on German soil and came under German domination. In 855 their King Rostislav freed them. In 863 he appealed to the Byzantine Emperor and to Patriarch Photius to send priests and missionaries who could teach the Moravians in their own language. Photius sent two famous brothers, Cyril and Methodius. Cyril (826-869), who was first named Constantine, and his brother, Methodius (815-885), were natives of Thessalonika. In their childhood they had learned the dialect of the Slavs around Thessalonika and could speak it fluently. They created a Slavonic alphabet and translated the liturgical books and the Bible into a language that was intelligible to the Moravians. That language has remained the liturgical language for all the Slavic Churches to this day.

What Cyril and Methodius accomplished cannot be overstated. They took the theology, philosophy and traditions of Byzantium and penetrated the unknown north which had not been Christianized yet. However, their attempts in Moravia failed because, although the Moravians spoke the Slavonic dialect, they had become accustomed to Latin as a liturgical language. Another reason for the failure was the close proximity of the Frankish States which were in consort with the Church of Rome. As we shall see, the work of Cyril and Methodius bore fruit in other Slavic areas.

THE SERBIANS

Possession of Thessalonika, a seaport of the Aegean Sea, had been the goal of every ruling power from the Danube River south. In the sixth century a Slavic group ventured past the Danube River and tried to sack Thessalonika but failed. Some turned back, but some remained. As a result, Slavic settlements sprang up all around the area. By the middle of the seventh century the entire upper Balkan peninsula was occupied by the Southern Slavs. At the time, Illyricum, a body of land on the western Balkan peninsula, was under the jurisdiction of Rome. Illyricum was a principal source of political conflict between Rome and Byzantium and played a major role in preparation for the Great Schism in 1054. Since the Province of Illyricum was in the hands of Rome at this time, Rome sent missionaries repeatedly to Christianize the Balkan Slavs, but each effort failed. The only Slavs who became Christians at this time were those who came into contact with the Eastern Christians of Thessalonika and its other coastal cities.

The few followers of Cyril and Methodius in Moravia were expelled, and they turned to Bulgaria, Serbia and later to Russia. A bishop was sent to Serbia and the Serbian Church began to grow. In the later Middle Ages the Serbian Nation expanded and spread to the Adriatic Sea. Under Sabbas, the Archbishop of all Serbia, monasteries were founded, churches were constructed and Byzantine art and iconography flourished. Sabbas became the Patron Saint for all Serbians.

THE BULGARIANS

The Bulgars, a mixture of Southern Slavs and a tribe of Hunnic origin, established themselves between the Danube River and the Black Sea in 680 A.D. The Bulgars became a Balkan Nation and soon established trade routes with the Byzantine Empire. The conversion of the Bulgarians came with King Boris (852-888), who asked Byzantine Emperor Michael III and Patriarch Photius in 863 for missionaires. The Bulgarian Church grew rapidly and in the middle of the tenth century was recognized as a Patriarchate. While Western Europe was still living in the Dark Ages, the Slavs in Bulgaria enjoyed a golden age of education, philosophy and theology.

THE ROMANIANS

Another Balkan Nation, Romania, was greatly influenced

by the work of Sts. Cyril and Methodius. The Romanians were of the Latin race, not Slavic. In the newly-organized Slavonic Churches bordering Romania this brought about a strange mixture of Latin and Slavonic terminology. The Romanian Orthodox Church borrowed heavily from the traditions and practices of the Slavic Churches influenced by Constantinople.

RUSSIA BECOMES ORTHODOX

Russia was initially called the Kievan State and was first exposed to Christianity through commercial caravans that traveled up and down the Dnieper River. The Russian people were also influenced by their neighboring states of Serbia and Bulgaria. The alphabet and Slavonic language of Sts. Cyril and Methodius infiltrated across the frontier borders and gave them a common language.

The prime mover for Russian Orthodox Christianity, however, was St. Vladimir *"Equal to the Apostles"* (980-1015). Vladimir sent a group of counselors to each of the major religious bodies (i.e., Judaism, Islam, Rome and Constantinople) to see how they actually worshipped in their own countries. When the counselors returned from Byzantium, remarking about the Divine Liturgy at St. Sophia, they said, *"We did not know whether we were on earth or in heaven."*

As a result, Vladimir visited Constantinople himself and was baptized in 987 A.D. In 988 the citizens of Kiev were baptized by the thousands in the Dnieper River. Christian schools were opened, monasteries were founded and missionaries were sent to the farthest corners of the nation. Churches were built and the services were conducted in the Slavonic language of Sts. Cyril and Methodius. Within a century, Orthodox Christianity reached the upper part of the Volga River. Both Vladimir and his grandmother, Olga, were proclaimed saints for their contribution to the Russian Orthodox Church.

CHAPTER TWELVE

DECLINE OF THE ROMAN EMPIRE

RISE OF THE PAPAL STATE

When Constantine the Great moved the capital of the Roman Empire to Byzantium, the West became isolated. Barbaric invasions of the fourth and fifth centuries brought the Goths (northern tribes) to Italy and Spain, the Gauls to France, and the Anglo-Saxons to England. Britain, France, Italy, North Africa and Spain all became Tribal States. The roads, coinage, postal system and all the other common and effective means of communications and administration of the Old Roman Empire were broken down. The political, economic and social orders disintegrated in the West. Economy became local and agricultural, as did mutual trade and bartering.

With decline and decay came a weakening of imperial central authority in the West. As time went on there was a silent drive or unity under one central authority, as there had been in previous years. Since the Byzantine Empire focused all its attention in the East, the lot fell to the Bishop of Rome as the central figure of unity. This did not happen overnight. It slowly developed between the sixth and tenth centuries. During this period of time the Bishop of Rome became a temporal ruler to whom the Tribal States in the West looked for guidance and direction. The gradual development of the political conditions, along with the doctrinal innovations, brought about this change. What emerged was the opposite of the autonomous Church administration known by the early **"One, Holy, Catholic and Apostolic Church."**

CONSOLIDATION OF THE PAPACY

One of the most significant developments during the decline of the Roman Empire in the West was the increasing prestige of the Bishops of Rome in both spiritual and temporal powers. The Bishops of Rome acquired sizeable strips of land both north and south of Rome, as well as in Sicily. They became magistrates of these properties. Soon they engaged in buying and selling, in shipping commodities and in going to war using their own armies.

POPE GREGORY THE GREAT (590-604)

Pope Gregory the Great best exemplified the Bishops of Rome during this period of time. A competent administrator, Gregory managed the estates of the Church so successfully that their revenues were increased. He raised armies and kept the Lombards out of Rome. He exercised authority in France and Spain and insisted on a primacy exclusive to the Bishop of Rome unheard of in the Early Church. Kenneth Scott Latourette, the eminent church historian writes: *"More than any other man, Gregory laid the foundation for the power which the Church of Rome was to exercise in the Western Europe of the next nine centuries."* A History of Christianity.

The seventh and eighth centuries brought even greater concentration of power in the Bishop of Rome, as the successor of St. Peter. By the ninth century, Papal Authority was defended on the basis of fabricated documents. But first, it is imperative to study the causes that precipitated the **Great Schism** of 1054 A.D.

DIFFERENCES RIGHT FROM THE BEGINNING

There were many differences between East and West right from the early centuries such as intellectual, ecccle-siastical, racial and political. But a unity in diversity prevailed so that the differences did not pose a threat of disunity and disharmony. With the transfer of the capital from Rome to Byzantium in the early fourth century the differences became acute. As the centuries progressed, there developed even greater differences between Byzantine and Latin customs and traditions. The Eastern

Patriarchs were subject to the authority of the Byzantine Emperors. Sometimes they had their support and sometimes they were suppressed by them. The position of the Patriarch, or Pope of Rome, as he came to be called, was entirely different, because he alone had jurisdiction in the Western world. Even though Rome was threatened, invaded and captured many times, with each recovery the Pope's position of authority increased. While the Eastern Bishops were under one unified Empire, the Bishop of Rome became the central leader figure for several Tribal Kingdoms. This gave him a special position of authority enjoyed by no other bishop. The fifth through seventh centuries noted the development of a Papal Supremacy that finally became fixed by the time of Pepin's Donation of Papal territory in the eighth century. The ninth century saw the beginning of the Holy Roman Empire which consisted of Italy, Germany, France and England. With the crowning of Charlamagne as Emperor of the Holy Roman Empire, the Pope of Rome added a new political dimension to his authority. The claim of Papal Supremacy, however, was built on more than political powers. It was argued on fabricated documents and doctrinal innovations which are imperative to know in order to understand how the **Great Schism** of 1054 came about.

DONATION OF CONSTANTINE AND THE FALSE ISIDORIAN DECRETALS

During the eighth century two forgeries were used to strengthen the authority of the Pope of Rome: The **Donation of Constantine** and the **Decretals of Isidore.** The former was an early fourth-century document describing Constantine the Great's conversion to Christianity, his baptism and his miraculous healing from leprosy by Pope Sylvester I. It is alleged that out of a deep sense of gratitude Constantine gave the Pope and all his successors his palace in Rome, as well as the City of Rome and all the provinces, districts and cities of the Western regions.

About the middle of the ninth century there arose the

Decretals of Isidore. The Apostles had passed on a series of instructions pertaining to sacraments, doctrines and administrative procedures. They were defined and approved as official documents at the First Ecumenical Council of 325. The Decretals (false rules and instructions), allegedly compiled by Isidore, Bishop of Seville (fifth century), depicted the Popes as claiming supreme authority from the beginning and requiring all bishops to appeal directly to the Pope for approval in all matters. On these two fabrications, Basil Stefanides, a contemporary Greek Orthodox historian comments and observes: *"No other forgery in the history of the world was accomplished with so much skill and no other had greater results."*

FILIOQUE CLAUSE

In the Creed issued by the First and Second Ecumenical Councils (Nicaea, 325 and Constantinople, 381), it is stated:

> ***"And (I believe) in the Holy Spirit, the Lord, the Giver of Life, who proceeds from the Father who together with the Father and the Son is worshipped and glorifed....."***

After ***"who proceeds from the Father"***, the Latin phrase ***"Filio que" (and the Son)*** was added in the Latin Creed. This practice first started in the seventh century in Toledo, Spain. To combat this alteration of the Creed and to admonish those using the *"Filioque,"* Pope Leo II in 794 ordered the Creed to be written on two silver plaques —in Greek and Latin— in its original form, and placed them in the Church of St. Peter in Rome. In spite of this, the *"Filioque"* clause began to spread throughout the Western Christian Church. It was one of the issues Charlamagne insisted on in his religious reform movement. It was first detected in 806 when the Greek monks heard Latin monks using it in the Divine Liturgy in Jerusalem. The *"Filioque"* clause may not appear at first to be significant. Nevertheless, it helped build and reinforce Papal Supremacy.

PETRINE PROMISE

The Roman Catholic Church believes that Papal Supremacy is documented in the Bible. Specifically, when Jesus asked an accounting from the Disciples after having sent them out to preach and perform miracles. Jesus asks:

> ***"'Who do men say that the Son of man is?' And they said, 'Some say John the Baptist, others say Elijah; and others Jeremiah or one of the prophets.' He said to them, 'But who do you say that I am?' Simon Peter replied, 'You are the Christ, the Son of the Living God.' And Jesus answered him, 'Blessed are you, Simon Bar-Jonah! For flesh and blood has not revealed this to you, but my Father Who is in Heaven. And I tell you, you are Peter, and on this rock I will build my Church, and the powers of death shall not prevail against it. I will give you the keys of the kingdom of heaven, and whatever you bind on earth shall be bound in heaven, and whatever you loose on earth shall be loosed in heaven'."*** (Matthew 16:13-19)

The Popes of Rome considered this passage as Jesus' personal call to Peter to succeed Him and be His representative on earth. The Orthodox Church does not take the same view as the Roman Catholic Church as regards these verses. We believe that when Peter spoke he represented all the disciples. Also,when Jesus answered him, he spoke not only to all the disciples, but to all the successive bishops of the Church throughout the centuries.

The Byzantine Church recognizes a universal primacy in the Roman Church, but it has nothing to do with the Bible. Sts. Peter and Paul both died in Rome, but this does not mean that the former was the first Bishop of Rome. St. Irenaeus said in the second century that Rome was a very great and ancient Church known to all. The famous 28th canon of the Fourth Ecumenical Council of Chalcedon (451) declared the Bishop of Rome to be the Bishop of a See with antiquity and respect, and to be regarded as the *"First Among Equals."* But the Roman Bishops never had a position of universal authority nor infallibility.

There is no evidence that the early Church knew of such an authority invested in the Bishop of Rome. Nor are there any patristic writings of the fourth to the eighth centuries to indicate the Church accepted the theory of a Petrine Promise. Essentially, this Bible quotation is a recognition by the Lord that St. Peter confessed Jesus Christ as the Son of God. The syntax is a play on words. Peter [masculine] was declared to be the *"petra"* [feminine], *"rock"* of the Church to the extent that he confessed this faith. Loosely translated, the Greek text says: *"You are Peter and on this rock-like faith witness commitment I will build my Church."* All those who make the same confession inherit the same promise. It is upon such confessions of believers that the Church is built. Furthermore, had Peter truly been the First Bishop of Rome, it is inconceivable that Paul would have ignored acknowledging his presence. (See Romans 15:20)

THE PETRINE PROMISE WITH THE FILIOQUE CLAUSE

The Filioque clause is fully understood with the Petrine Promise. The First and Second Ecumenical Councils used certain words and phrases to describe how man could understand the doctrine of the Holy Trinity. One of the doctrinal statements was that the Holy Spirit is the ***"Giver of Life"***, which works through the Sacraments and the grace of the Church. After Jesus' resurrection, He promised the disciples He would ask God the Father to send the Holy Spirit at the appointed time (Pentecost Sunday). The Filioque clause with the Petrine Promise would imply that if Jesus can send the Holy Spirit —and Jesus ostensibly asks Peter to be His Vicar, His successor and representative on earth- then Peter, too, can send the

Holy Spirit. And if Peter is the First Bishop of Rome then he, too, has both the power and authority to send the Holy Spirit. It follows then, that each consecutive Bishop of Rome is also Christ's Vicar and Representative on earth. Therefore the Pope of Rome has sole and sovereign authority and is above reproach in all matters. This false teaching solidified Papal authority to an unbelievable degree.

PAPAL SUPREMECY FIXED.

By the early tenth century the false notion of Papal Supremacy became fixed. Papal Supremacy, coupled with political issues and territorial expansion of the Papal State, played a major role in the division of the Church. When these were imposed upon the East they brought about the **Great Schism** in 1054 A.D. The culmination of Papal Supremacy, however, was perhaps best described by Pope Gregory VII, called Hildebrand (1073-1085), when he defined the Papal position in 27 affirmations, among which the following stand out:

> *"The Roman Church was founded by God; the Roman Pontiff alone deserves the title 'Ecumenical'; he alone can depose or reinstate bishops; he may transfer a bishop from one See to another; he has the power to ordain a cleric of any Church and he who is ordained by him may not receive a higher grade from any other bishop; no Synod can be called Ecumenical without his authorization; a sentence passed by him cannot be reversed by anyone except himself; he may be judged by no one; to him should be referred the important cases of every Church; the Roman Church has never erred, nor will it to all eternity; he who is not at peace with the Roman Church shall not be considered Catholic; the Roman Pontiff may absolve subjects from their allegiance to wicked men."*

CHAPTER THIRTEEN

THE GREAT SCHISM

THE PHOTIAN SCHISM

The ninth century was a unique century because both the Holy Roman Empire (West) and the Byzantine Empire (East) were on the upswing. The Byzantine Empire attained its highest point since the beginning of the Arab conquests. It was during this period of time that ecclesiastical authority fell upon two eminently powerful churchmen: Patriarch Photius of Constantinople and Pope Nicholas I of Rome. It had become a traditional practice for the five Patriarchal Bishops of Jerusalem, Antioch, Alexandria, Rome and Constantinople to exchange announcement greetings upon their election and enthronement. When Photius ascended the Throne of Constantinople in 861, Nicholas refused to recognize him claiming that he had not been consulted. Ignatius, Photius' predecessor, was deposed and Nicholas sent two representatives to investigate. When they reported everything had been in order and proper, Pope Nicholas refused to accept their decision. He called a council in Rome in 863 and stripped Photius of his title and reinstated Ignatius. Nicholas asserted Papal prerogatives and declared that through Him Christ Himself was speaking. This was clearly the first official and public declaration of Papal Supremacy in Constantinople. Both the Emperor and Patriarch Photius ignored the intervention.

Another controversy arose between Nicholas and Photius. King Boris of Bulgaria asked Photius to send missionaries to Christianize the Bulgarians. However, Boris wanted both an independent church and an independent state. When he got no response to his requests, Boris then turned to Pope Nicholas, who responded favorably but for different reasons. The Pope sent his own bishops and priests, who expelled all the Eastern clergy and introduced Latin customs. They also imposed the Creed with the **Filioque** clause. Photius called a Council in Constantinople in 867 to condemn this anticanonical (illegal) act of Pope Nicholas. Representatives of Antioch, Jerusalem and Alexandria participated in this council which excommunicated Nicholas. This first mutual schism between East and West came to be known as the **Photian Schism.** Another Council was held in Constantinople in 879, at which papal representatives participated and retracted the excommunications, and Pope John VIII officially recognized Photius as the rightful Patriarch of Constantinople, thus ending the Photian Schism.

THE ONE, HOLY, CATHOLIC AND APOSTOLIC CHURCH IS TORN ASUNDER

The Byzantine Empire enjoyed one of the most brilliant periods of its long and glorious history during the ninth through the eleventh centuries. Constantinople dominated the Mediterranean world with wealth, culture and artistic achievement. Conversely, in Western Europe the Dark Ages set in. Those were the years of ignorance, immorality and degradation. With the eleventh century a group of Cluniac monks set out to reform the Roman Catholic Church. Pope Leo IX (1048-1054), a product of the Cluniac reform movement, succeeded in strengthening the authority of the Popes, enforced celibacy upon the clergy, and insisted on the Filioque clause. Leo IX also extended his reform movement to Southern Italy and Sicily, which were under the jurisdiction of Constantinople. He deposed clergy and closed churches that did not conform to his demands. Patriarch Michael Cerularius of Constantinople, upon hearing of this, protested. The scene is now set for the **Great Schism.**

DEMANDS OF POPE LEO IX

When Patriarch Michael learned what Leo IX was doing in Southern Italy, he closed Latin Rite churches and monasteries in the East. Pope Leo dispatched a letter to Byzantine Emperor Constantine IX Monomachos and Patriarch Michael Cerularius in which he asserted these Papal claims: Christ's commission to St. Peter (Petrine Promise), the Donation of Constantine and Papal Supremacy over the entire Church. Wanting to keep an harmonious relationship, the Emperor and the Patriarch sent a moderate reply. Leo interpreted their responses as arrogant and prepared another letter in which he asserted total supremacy and demanded complete and total obedience.

THE BULL OF EXCOMMUNICATION

Pope Leo IX sent his letter to Emperor Constantine IX Monomachos with Cardinal Humbert (a Cluniac monk), Archbishop Frederick of Lorraine (and Chancellor to the Papal Office), and Bishop Peter of Amalfi. The legates arrived in Constantinople early in 1054 but met only with the Emperor, refusing to meet with the Patriarch. The legates insisted on the papal demands of Leo IX. In the meantime, the Normans invaded Rome and made a prisoner of Pope Leo IX, where he died in April of 1054. Rightfully, the legates were no longer empowered to represent the Pope. All action should have been suspended until the election of a new Pope, but Cardinal Humbert and the other two legates continued to make their demands. The Patriarch refused to make any concessions to the Papal legates or to the See of Rome, contending that the claims were unfounded and contrary to the tradition, practice and history of the Church.

After several months the Papal representatives decided that they could not negotiate with the Byzantines. On Saturday, July 16, 1054, while Patriarch Michael Cerularius was celebrating the Divine Liturgy in St. Sophia, the legates entered the church and deposited the Bull of Excommunication on the holy altar table. The Papal Bull said:

"Michael (Cerularius) and his followers, along with all the heretics, guilty of the above mentioned errors and insolences, together with the devil and his angels shall be considered anathema [cut off from the Church]."

THE SCHISM BECOMES FINAL

Within a few days after the Bull of Excommunication, Patriarch Michael called a Council in Constantinople and excommunicated the legates. The Patriarchates of Jerusalem, Antioch and Alexandria, upon being notified, supported Michael Cerularius and remained loyal to the Church of the East. Thus the **One, Holy, Catholic and Apostolic Church** was torn asunder because Papal Supremacy, which at first took over and was contained in the West, was finally imposed upon the East. At first the Schism seemed to be a local issue that would resolve itself, as did the Photian Schism and other disputes. But the two sides were further separated by the irritations and differences which continued. However, that which decisively cemented the separation between East and West were the Four Crusades.

THE CRUSADES

In the latter part of the eleventh century, Pope Urban II promoted the First Crusade to free the Holy Lands from the Arabs. There were two ways for the Crusaders to go from Western Europe to the Holy Lands: By land or by sea. In either case, they had to come in contact with the Orthodox Christians in the East. Wherever they went they made every attempt possible to Latinize the clergy and laity. The greatest blow struck when, in 1204 A.D., the Fourth Crusade turned to Constantinople instead of Jerusalem. The Latin conquerors of Constantinople replaced the Patriarch with a Latin Prelate. They did the same in Antioch and Jerusalem. The Byzantine Emperor, the Patriarch, Clergy and Laity who did not submit to Latin practices were forced to seek exile in Nicaea, the city where the First Ecumenical Council took place. The Latin Crusaders stayed for some sixty years, when another Byzantine Emperor recaptured Constantinople in 1261 A.D. Eastern Patriarchs were restored to Constantinople, Antioch and Jerusalem. Thus what seemed to have been but a temporary problem just a few years before had now become a complete and total Schism between the See of Rome and Western Christians, and the Eastern Patriarchates of Constantinople, Antioch, Jerusalem and Alexandria, as well as Eastern Christendom.

CONSEQUENCES OF THE CRUSADES

Steven Runciman, a contemporary Byzantine scholar, who has written three volumes on the Crusades, writes:

"The harm done by the Crusades to Islam was small in comparison with that done by them to Eastern Christendom. Pope Urban II had bidden the Crusades go forth that the Christians of the East might be helped and rescued. It was a strange rescue; for when the work was over, Eastern Christendom lay under infidel domination and the Crusaders themselves had done all that they could to prevent its recovery." (History of Crusaders Vol. III.)

The greatest tragedy that was revealed by the Period of the Crusades is that Western Christendom never really comprehended Byzantium. They came to look upon the Byzantine Christians as adversaries, just as they had the infidels. And what is even more significant, they intensified the hatred and scorn of the Muslims for the Christian name. Byzantium will survive another two hundred years once they return to the city of Constantinople. However, it will no longer be a normal life, but a slow, agonizing death. The Crusaders will have undermined its effective resistance against the Turks. When the Ottoman Turks, the most menacing and fiercest of all the Sultanates, finally come in the middle of the fifteenth century, they will come to stay.

CHAPTER FOURTEEN

THE RESULTS OF THE GREAT SCHISM

Over nine hundred years have passed since the occurrence of the greatest calamity in the History of the Church; namely, the **Great Schism of 1054!** Many factors brought about the Schism, but the most significant are the **Cultural, Political** and **Theological.**

CULTURAL CAUSES

The Cultural Causes are perhaps the most difficult to explain, because they are the sociological and psychological factors which are not too easily perceived. They are not as apparent as the political and theological ones. And yet, they played a dominant role in the Schism.

There was a fundamental difference in Greek and Latin temperaments which dated back to the beginning of Christianity. Up to the year 200 A.D.,Greek was the language of the Church in both East and West. It served as a means of theological expression and as a universal language of communication. With the turn of the third century, Latin became the spoken and scholarly language of the West.

The East was interested in philosophy, speculative thought and mysticism --all of which were inherited from the Hellenistic Period. The Church Fathers emphasized a Jesus Christ Who was resurrected, Who was to be imitated, Who was to be met on a heavenly plain. The basic theological teachings were defined in the Ecumenical Councils, all of which were convened in the East. The vast majority of the Christian writers of the Golden Age were from the East. The Divine Liturgy in the East sought to elevate man, or as the late Dr. Nikos Nissiotis, eminent Orthodox theologican put it so eloquently, ***"Orthodoxy is to live in the glory of God and not in the misery of man!"*** The West, on the other hand, was not interested in philosophy until the period of Scholasticism, in the twelfth and thirteenth centuries.

With the exception of St. Clement of Rome, St. Cyprian of Carthage and St. Augustine of Hippo, there were but a few Western theologians before the eleventh century. The West was more concerned with concise, legalistic and institutional practices which were inherited from the Romans. The emphasis was on the Crucified, Suffering Christ, Whose Passion was to be dwelt upon. As the centuries developed, the Passion was overemphasized and the deification of man in God's saving grace was de-emphasized.

The fourth and fifth centuries showed an even more dramatic cultural separation with the rise of the Byzantine Empire and the decline of political and central authority in Rome. In the East, the Church maintained a uniformity and control in her expansion and growth. With the transfer of the capital to Byzantium, the West experienced a decay and breakdown. Barbaric tribes of Goths, Gauls, Germans and Anglo-Saxons invaded the Western part of the empire. Added to the diverse temperaments, the breakup of the Western Empire brought about a formation of Tribal States with political power, which gradually isolated them from the Byzantine Empire. There was also an inherent rivalry between Rome and Byzantium. These are the intangible factors and causes which contributed to the development of the Great Schism.

POLITICAL CAUSES

The Political Causes were equally important in the accumulation of problems which led to the Great Schism. The Western Empire began its decline and decay in the fourth and fifth centuries. The Church of Rome became the sole unifying force and center for the West. All the other Churches in the West looked to Rome for guidance and direction. With each century that passed, the newly-created Roman City-State grew in geographic size and increased in political strength. By the sixth and seventh centuries, the political authority vested in the

Bishop of Rome was becoming fixed in the West. This was first noted when Justinian the Great designated Ravenna the Exarchate for the Western part of the Byzantine Empire. Up to this time the Bishop of Rome considered himself a subject of the Byzantine throne. The designation of the Ravenna Exarchate gave the Bishop of Rome an independence that grew with time into a prestige of primacy.

The eighth century noted a second significant political factor when the Bishop of Rome supported the Iconodules against Emperor Leo the Isaurian, who was an Iconoclast. Although Leo punished him by removing the Illyricum Province [see below] from Roman jurisdiction and placing it in the jurisdiction of the Byzantine Patriarch, this is the first time a Roman Bishop expressed open defiance against the Byzantine Emperor. The third and final strike at independence was when Pope Stephen II crossed the Alps and made a pact with Pepin. He crowned Pepin King of the Franks and all Germanic tribes and in return Pepin defeated the advancing Lombards. Pepin not only safeguarded Rome but gave a vast body of land to the Pope, thus expanding Papal territory. To these territories must be added the Feudal acquisition of lands over which not only Popes, but European Bishops and Abbots of Monasteries were lords. Some Bishops assumed titles of duke and baron along with their ecclesiastical titles. These conditions and circumstances were not found among the Hierarchy and Clergy of the East. There were strong Bishops and weak Bishops in the East, but they were always bishops, not rulers with temporal and earthly authority. There simply was no parallel of sovereign rule in any of the Eastern Patriarchates as there was in Rome.

The final political cause was found in the Province of Illyricum, that part of the Balkan peninsula which had become a political football passed back and forth between Byzantium and Rome. It was a strategic body of land that was coveted by barbaric tribes as well as civilized nations throughout the history of the Church. It alone, more than any other geographical area, played the most consequential political role in all the historical conflicts that nourished the seeds of the Great Schism. [Ironically, it was in the Illyricum Province, that Balkan peninsula, that the First World War began; and it remains to this day a political and strategic area for both the Republic of Russia and the Western Powers.]

THEOLOGICAL CAUSES

The first of the theological causes which must be considered is the Donation of Constantine, which was fabricated and allegedly gave the Bishop of Rome the title of *"Pontiff and Father of the Universe."* The second was the document called *"False Isidorian Decretals,"* which allegedly stated the rules outlining the authority and supremacy of the Pope of Rome. Third was the *"Filioque Clause"* which was based on the personal promise of Jesus Christ to St. Peter, and to each subsequent Bishop of Rome, to be His sole representative on earth. This false doctrine gave way not only to the theory of supremecy, but to the false doctrine of **"Papal Infallibility,"** too. All of these define a position for the Bishop of Rome which was unknown in the Early Christian Church, and one which the Patriarchs of the East simply could not accept!

ATTEMPTS AT REUNION

There were numerous attempts to reunite East and West. Out of all of them only three actually brought about a form of union, but they were never accepted by the people. The first one, of course, was during the Fourth Crusade in 1204 when Constantinople was sacked and pillaged, and the Greek clergy were forced to submit to the union or leave. The second was the so-called Union of Lyons in 1274, and the third was the Council of Florence-Ferrara in 1438-1439. In the first instance Emperor Michael VIII Paleologus wanted Pope Gregory X to stop Charles of Anjou from further advancing on the Byzantine Empire and threatening to capture Constantinople. In the second, Emperor John VIII Paleologus wanted a papal army and supplies to help ward off the fast advancing Ottoman Turks. The Popes wanted to secure a union, but on their own terms; that is to say, total submission to the Pope of Rome. Each attempt at reunion between East and West invariably was predicated on political and coercive reasons and not doctrinal ones. Therefore, the clergy and laity rejected them; and they did not succeed.

ARCHBISHOP MARK EUGENICUS

While most of the Eastern delegates to the Council of Florence-Ferrara signed the union, it was Mark Eugenicus, Archbishop of Ephesus, who both defended the Orthodox Faith and refused to sign. When Pope Eugenius IV heard Mark had not signed, he said, *"If Mark has not signed, we have accomplished nothing!"* When the delegates returned to the East, the clergy and laity rejected the union and embraced the position of Mark Eugenicus.

SUMMARY

The Orthodox Church has a rich heritage of Tradition and a legacy of culture, art, literature and history. To be sure, there were occasions in the East when Christian virtue and morals were at a low ebb. There were events which emphasized the ethnic relations and de-emphasized the religious spirit of the Church our Lord founded. If there is one single element in the Orthodox Church that is beyond reproach, it is that the cultural, political and theological events of history have not distorted nor falsified the basic doctrines of the **One, Holy, Catholic and Apostolic Church** handed down from Jesus Christ and His Apostles. No segment of the Orthodox Church imposed supremacy upon any other Church throughout history.

Union presents many stumbling blocks that will require serious-minded theological deliberations. Pope Leo IX's Bull of Excommunication delivered by Cardinal Humbert and his colleagues, and the counter excommunication by

Patriarch Michael Cerularius, were mutually lifted by Patriarch Athenagoras I and Pope Paul VI in 1965. Archbishop Iakovos stated to the press on December 30, 1965:

> *"The lifting of the Excommunication Ban cannot be interpreted as nullifying the Schism between the Churches of the East and the West. That which took place in this instance was simply a mutual gesture of good will between the two Churches."*

The greatest stumbling block between Roman Catholics and Orthodox remains a primacy which is miscontrued to mean a Supremacy and Infallibility of the Bishop of Rome. We recognize the primacy of honor given to him by the early church. We reject the supremacy demanded!

In conclusion, it must be stated that a desire for reunion is not enough. Ecumenism, Ecumenical Movement and reunion do not mean a *"Return to Rome,"* nor a *"Return to Byzantium,"* nor a return to Luther, Calvin and the fifteenth-century reformers, for that matter. The Orthodox attitude concerning reunion is an appeal to all Churches to *"return"* to the Orthodoxy and Tradition of the **"One, Holy, Catholic and Apostolic Church"** from which all sprang. It means a *"return"* to the Patristic theology. This does not mean that we should not be friendly and work for common Christian goals with our fellow Christians. We have much to learn from each other, and we must seek ways and means to discuss and overcome our differences. This is Christian Unity; and we should continue to strive for it, because this will prepare the way for Christian Union. But we should not mistake one for the other, nor should we sacrifice one for the other.

Roman Catholics, Protestants and Orthodox have come a long way in ecumenical relations. However, the basic doctrines and fundamental differences which separated us in the first place are still there. These must be resolved before before reunion can take place.

CHAPTER FIFTEEN

SCHOLASTICISM IN THE WEST

During the three centuries in which the Four Crusades occurred, Western Europe underwent a period of intellectual curiosity which led to the establishment of different types of Schools. Prior to this time, the Guild Schools, schools which taught the traders and crafts needed for everyday living, were the only ones the West had available for any other than the clergy. Education was generally confined to the clergy and an elite few. The twelfth century ushered in an era of intellectual knowledge for the West. Many universities opened, and a multitude of students began to devote themselves to the study of theology and philosophy. The methods they used --philosophical arguments to teach and learn theology-came to be called **Scholasticism.**

Scholasticism is derived from the Greek word *schole*, school. A scholastic was a student taught in the university. Scholasticism became a method through which a teacher guided students in learning about God, creation, the universe, man and salvation, by applying the pattern of questioning, debating and finally, the forming of conclusions. This was the pattern used by the ancient Greek philosophers, Plato and Aristotle. The teacher used three principal sources as a base and authority: The **Holy Bible,** the **Church Fathers** and **Hellenistic philosophy.**

The basic method of scholasticism was not new. It had been used in earlier centuries by the Patristic Fathers. But they pursued this avenue of approach only to a point and then stopped, for fear they might present a theology alien to what Jesus Christ and the Holy Apostles taught. Scholasticism set out to blend logical reasoning with the Christian Faith. But as it grew, it extended far beyond the boundaries of religion. Scholasticism attempted to resolve all the questions of life, whether these pertained to religion, politics, economics or the supernatural. Since Scholasticism played such a major role in the Roman

Catholic and Protestant Churches, it is necessary to discuss briefly the Orthodox response to Scholasticism.

THE ORTHODOX CHURCH AND SCHOLASTICISM

The Christian East was the first to employ Hellenistic thought in understanding and clarifying the teachings of the Church. The Cappadocian Fathers (St. Basil the Great, St. Gregory of Nyssa and St. Gregory of Nazianzus) used Hellenistic philosophical thoughts to help them understand our relationship with God better. But there is no historical evidence that Scholasticism either affected or influenced Eastern doctrine in the way it did in the West. To be sure, man is challenged to reach his intellectual potential through education, knowledge and personal experience. But at some point he has to realize his inadequacies, his inability and his lack of full comprehension of God's truths, at least in this life. It is precisely at this point that we must place our trust and faith in God and await enlightenment through the grace of the Holy Spirit.

Scholasticism attempted to explain all things, even to the point of theorizing just how many angels could fit on the head of a pin. The great hazard in Scholastic theology became apparent in theorizing how God thinks and acts. For example, if God knows everything --past, present and future-- if He knows even before we do something that we are going to do it, then we can't help doing it. If we can't help doing it, then it must be prearranged. The logical extension of this type of Scholastic thought finally developed in Calvanistic predestination which came about after the Protestant Reformation. Calvanist predestination taught that there are two classes of people in the world: **Elect** and **Non-elect.** That is to say, those who are predestined to be saved and those who are not. While this will be discussed in greater detail in a later chapter, suffice it to say that Scholasticism expressed itself in a way that there was no turning back for the West to the ancient Patristic tradition. Roman Catholicism emphasized the rational approach at the expense of mystery and faith. Protestantism, on the other hand, completely abandoned mystery and took over the rational approach. However, to limit ourselves to the Church of Rome for the moment, any number of examples can be given:

The Eucharistic Supper

The Eucharistic Supper, the Divine Liturgy, is a classic example of how Scholasticism deviated from the ancient Patristic tradition. The West tried to define in minute detail how the bread and wine become the Body and Blood of Jesus Christ. They did this by qualifying what the outer appearances are in terms of physical and organic matter [bread and wine] and the inner substance in terms of philosophical formulae and theory. The Latin word *substantia (substance)* was used for the Greek word *ousia*, which is better translated as essence in English. Scholasticism tried to explain how the inner substance of the bread and wine actually change in a way understandable and describable by the human mind.

The East simply took Jesus at His word when He said, ***"This is My Body...This is My Blood."*** With the utterance of the Epiklesis, the Prayer of Invocation which asks the Father to send down the Holy Spirit and change the bread and wine into the Body and Blood of Christ, the Orthodox Christian accepts: a) That outwardly the Gifts still appear as bread and wine; and b) That inwardly, in some mysterious, miraculous and unexplainable way, the bread and wine are truly the Body and Blood of Jesus Christ which we receive for the remission of sins and for ever-lasting life.

The theological term used to describe this mysterious and miraculous change in the

Eastern Liturgy is the Greek word, *metousiosis. Metousiosis* means a change in the essence without necessarily defining it nor logically explaining it. The Latin West took this word and translated it into Latin as *transubstantia*, out of which developed the Scholastic theology of Transubstantiation. This is the word used to define, describe and explain how in the Roman Catholic Eucharist the bread and wine change into the Body and Blood of Christ.

The Orthodox East is satisfied with Jesus' words without fully comprehending them, when He says: ***"I am the bread of life....I am the living bread which came down from heaven; if anyone eats of this bread, he will live forever; and the bread which I shall give for the life of the world is my flesh...Truly, I say to you, unless you eat the flesh of the Son of Man and drink His blood, you have no life in you; he who eats my flesh and drinks my blood has eternal life, and I will raise him up at the last day. For my flesh is food indeed, and my blood is drink indeed. He who eats my flesh and drinks my blood abides in me, and I in him."*** *(John 6:48-56)*

The Church

The West regards the Church as an Earthly Institution which brings God on earth to rule the world. The Divine Liturgy, the Sacraments, worship services, each of these is understood in terms of God descending upon earth and ruling through the Church, as an Institution. This kind of Church is justified in setting up laws and rules to govern the world. Any number of examples can be given to illustrate how the Medieval Latin Church reacted to scientific discoveries. This type of Church conceives itself as an Institution that sends its tentacles out to govern and control all aspects of society: Education, politics, morality, social conscience, etc. But the Church was involved in Feudalism, Wars, the Industrial Revolution, Social Inequalities and a host of injustices.

The Orthodox East also regards the Church as a Divine Institution, but not in the same way as the Latin West. We believe the Church elevates us to a heavenly dimension where through the Holy Spirit we are united with Jesus Christ. He enlightens us, inspires us and graces our lives, and then returns us to earth where we are to go out and influence society in all its aspects and phases. Whereas the West regards the Church as the structured organization to do this, the East considers Church members the ones to restore God's ruling power on earth as it is in heaven. This takes the onus of responsibility off of God and puts it squarely on our shoulders.

Man

The West regards man as a creation of God who was made perfect in the absolute sense. But through sin man cut himself off from God and fell into a state of total depravity where there was nothing he could do but await the mercy and love of God to redeem him. With the Coming of Jesus Christ man is restored, but he has to depend solely upon God's grace and mercy.

The East regards man as the reflection and image of God, who was created perfect in the potential sense. That is to say, he has the faculties to perfect himself in due time. Although man fell away from God as a result of sin, he was not cut off from God completely. His distance from God clouded his

reflection and image in God. With Christ, man is restored to the point where he originally was, however with the difference that he now still has the temptation and capacity to sin again. Through the sacramental life of the Church man can utilize his knowledge, experience and personal faith. He can join his energies with God's saving grace through the Holy Spirit and be saved. To be sure, man needs God's grace and mercy, but he also must have the determination, will and motivation to bring about his salvation. We would say:

Objectively, we are saved fully and completely through the saving grace of Jesus Christ which we receive freely from Him.

Subjectively, we must accept the salvation which Jesus Christ gives us freely through faith and by living a Christlike life in this world.

In other words, God wills our salvation, but we must want it!

Although these fundamental differences were slowly developing in the West from the sixth through the eleventh centuries, they became formalized and crystallized during the Age of Scholasticism. They were first introduced by the West at the Council of Lyons in 1274, where they were received as points of view totally foreign to the traditional Patristic patterns. They were later presented and declared as true doctrines with authority at the Council of Florence-Ferrara in 1439. However, by the fifteenth century the influence of Scholasticism had become fixed in the West; and there was no longer a meeting of the minds between East and West.

CHAPTER SIXTEEN

THE RENAISSANCE PERIOD IN THE WEST

Renaissance is a French word that means to be born again, rebirth or revival. Specifically, it is a period of time in Western European history that took place during the fourteenth, fifteenth and sixteenth centuries. This was a period of time when the ancient Greek and Roman classics were revived in the West and when a realistic and naturalistic type of expression was introduced in the arts, education and culture. There are two principal causes generally accepted for the dawning of the Renaissance:

1) Byzantium and the Muslim world had cultivated a mercantile trade throughout the Mid-East and had opened both long and short haul trade routes with the Far East and China. With the onslaught of the Crusades, especially the Fourth Crusade of 1204-1261, Westerners were exposed to the theory of a profit-sharing economy, an economic theory totally unknown to most Europeans who lived under the Feudal System. As will be recalled, the Feudal System allowed for only two classes: Landowners and indentured servants. Although there were a few artisans and skilled craftsmen they did not work on a profit-making basis as we know and understand it. The first to recognize the importance of mercantile trade were the City-States of Italy, such as Venice, Florence, Genoa, Naples and Pisa The Italian mercantile trade gradually developed and spread throughout Western Europe.

2) The other reason for the Renaissance, perhaps more subtle and less noticeable, was the gradual awakening of ethnic consciousness, a spirit of nationalism throughout the

City-States. Attempts had been made earlier by Charlamagne (eighth century) and other monarchs to unify all the territories of Europe. Germans began to have a sense of pride and spirit for German nationalism. French, English, Spanish, Portuguese and Italians followed the same pattern. The monarchs, nobility, mercantile class and peasantry no longer thought in terms of one central authority, whether it be in Rome or anywhere else. State Universities emerged with the support and protection of princes and nobility where the vernacular language came into use and superseded Latin in literary works.

HUMANISM

One of the most apparent facets of the Renaissance Period is the concept of Humanism. Humanism, as it developed during the Renaissance, means an excessive preoccupation with the nature of man, his reaction and response as a part of nature. Humanism found its expression in literature, painting and sculpturing with a focus on secular themes. Unlike the Scholastics who preocupied themselves with the philosophy of life, the Humanists concentrated their attention upon the natural world surrounding them. They stressed the task of observing nature in all its splendor and describing it in a classic style.

RENAISSANCE ART

Humanism played its most important role in art, painting and sculpture. In sculpture the attention of the artist was focused on the natural and human lines of the body (muscler, tone, shape, form, expression, etc.). In painting, whereas the visual presentation had been restricted primarily to religious themes before, it now emphasized secular scenes and subjects from pagan mythology and contemporary events of living persons. Where golden settings had formerly been used as a background, the Humanist artists now enlivened their paintings with naturalistic scenes. They depicted meadows, woods, lakes, mountains, skies, flowers, birds and beasts. They also depicted human beings carrying on their varied activities in country and town, in trade and agriculture, in war, peace and love.

RENAISSANCE AND MORAL DECAY OF THE PAPACY

Although the Renaissance Period offered innumerable contributions in art, culture and learning, it also contributed to the deterioration of the moral fibre of the Roman Church. As advocates of Humanism emphasized more and more the importance of nature and the subject of man, ambitious men hungry for power and luxury worked their way in the Papal Court and the College of Cardinals. By the end of the fifteenth century, the Papacy reached its lowest depth of moral degradation. Pope Innocent VIII (1484-1492), an individual who had been a pawn of Renaissance Humanistic thought, was in urgent need of income. He began selling Church positions, that is to say, Bishops' Sees, Abbeys, etc. He also created new ones which he sold as well. Some of his appointments were highly questionable and scandalizing to the faithful. For example, he appointed Giovanni de Medici, a twelve year old lad, Abbot of the famous Benedictine Mother House, Monte Cassino. He later became a Cardinal at the age of sixteen --evidence of the deterioration of both the Papacy and Monasticism in the West.

Several Cardinals lived in excessive luxury in the style of the secular princes and the wealthy families. Others who held key positions in the Church helped to undermine the trust and confidence in the Church. Ironically during this time the Italian Humanist Lorenzo Valla, while he held the post of papal secretary, prepared an historical research paper, using scientific investigation and textual criticism, in which he proved the so-called fourth century *"Donation of Constantine"* to be a forged document.

Some of the Popes, such as Nicholas V (1447-1455), Pius II (1458-1464), Julius II (1503-1513) and Leo X (1513-1521) displayed little or no interest in theology or the Church. And although they bestowed patronage upon some of the most brilliant artists and literary men of the Renaissance, they contributed greatly to the moral decay of the Roman Church. In fact, these four Popes did more to bring about the Protestant Reformation than did the Reformers themselves!

CONCLUSION

In our attempt to illustrate the Orthodox Christian East as the historical, doctrinal and traditional Church of the first ten centuries, we must be very careful not to overlook the magnificent contributions of the Christian West. The Renaissance Period cannot be ignored as though it never occurred. Great was the contribution and the legacy which emanated from the art, culture and beauty of the Renaissance. However, the Renassiance, especially in its Humanistic approach, did more to contribute to the scandal and deterioration of the Christian Church in the West than any other force. Humanism reflected itself in worship, doctrine and religious art. As beautiful as Renaissance art is, it still overemphasizes the human aspect of man at the expense of his spirituality and relationship with God. Renaissance art tends to humanize God, Christ, the saints and man. Byzantine iconography strives to emphasize the divinity of God. The purpose is to convey both the divinity and humanity of Christ Who was both God and Man, but Who overcame the world To depict the saints in a way that represent what human man and woman can accomplish **with** God's saving grace.

Renaissance Humanism gives man the excuses he needs to cover up his faults, sins and shortcomings, whereas Orthodox theology gives him a prototype and example he can follow and imitate. Surely the greatest example is Christ Himself. Renaissance Humanism illustrates and

emphasizes the Suffering, Crucified Jesus Christ in all His agony and pain, whereas Orthodox Christianity emphasizes the Eternally Resurrected Jesus Christ Who encourages us to endure, Who shows us the way, Who elevates and lifts us up to His heavenly dimension. The former leaves us hopeless while the latter gives us great hope.

Another illustration is the dramatic contrast in how the Resurrection of our Lord and Savior Jesus Christ is depicted in the West and in the East. The Renaissance Humanist painting of Christ's Resurrection depicts Him with a white tunic and holding a banner with cross while floating on a heavenly white cloud. The Orthodox Byzantine icon of the Resurrection is quite different. Christ is depicted standing on the gates of hell which He has torn asunder through His Death and Resurrection. We proclaim this triumphant event over and over in the magnificent Orthodox Easter Pascha hymn: *"Christ is risen from the dead, Death trampling down upon death, bestowing life to those in the tombs!"* Jesus is shown reaching down into Hell and pulling up Adam and Eve, and all their descendents, up to the thieves on Golgotha, offering them salvation and eternal life! We relive this awesome event on Holy Saturday morning in Orthodox Churches all over the world and liturgically call it *"The First Resurrection."* This is called the *"Theology of the Middle Day,"* between Good Friday and Easter Pascha. The Easter Pascha Resurrection Liturgy for us takes place at midnight, Saturday night.

CHAPTER SEVENTEEN

DECLINE OF THE PAPACY

CONCILIAR MOVEMENT IN THE WEST

The world at the beginning of 1300 was quite different from 1095 when the First Crusade began. With the Crusades Western Europe was exposed to the Byzantine East with its refinements, culture and art. Add to these the establishment of universities, the emergence of new nations and the outpouring of lectures, books and pamphlets in the vernacular. All these created a new atmosphere and environment in the West. The Papacy also flourished during this period of time and exerted much power and influence. Toward the end of the thirteenth century, the Christian West found itself at its peak of power. Papal authority was recognized as supreme throughout Western Europe.

At the same time, however, other things were taking place which were too subtle to be noticed: Rulers wanted more power; individuals emerged who questioned the authority of papal supremacy; and a movement arose which advocated a shift from central papal authority to a conciliar authority. This meant that decisions which were binding on the Church should be made by representative delegate bishops and not by an authoritative decree from the papal throne. As all this came about the strength of the papacy began to decline.

THE PAPACY

When Boniface VIII became Pope in 1294, he attempted to pursue the role as his predecessors; but he antagonized the nobility, challenged the rights of the Kings, and excommunicated those who disagreed with him. In 1302 he issued a papal bull called *"Unam Sanctam,"* in which he not only asserted full papal jurisdictional rights, but also put forward general claims to supreme authority in secular (civil) as well as spiritual matters. The French and English Kings rejected Boniface's claims and demanded that a council of Bishops be called to question his authority with the ultimate purpose to censure him. Pope Boniface died before the council was called. Pope Clement V was elected in 1305 and moved the Papal Throne to Avignon, France, where it remained for the next seventy years.

TWO POPES REIGN SIMULTANEOUSLY

In 1377, Pope Gregory XI attempted to reestablish papal residence in Rome but he died the following year. His successor, Urban IV, continued the residency in Rome; but he antagonized the cardinals, and they elected another Pope to replace him. Clement VII, the new Pope, returned to Avignon, while Urban IV remained in Rome. Now the West had two Popes simultaneously: One in Rome and one in Avignon. Each insisted *he* was the canonical Pope and each issued papal bulls, decrees, excommunications. Each also made treaties and pacts with monarchs and nobility. This not only split the Western Church, but divided nations on the basis of their political interests.

(1) Spain, France, Scotland and part of Germany supported the Avignon Pope.

(2) Northern and Central Italy, most of Germany, England, Scandanavia, Bohemia, Poland, Flanders and Portugal remained with Rome. This furthered the development and growth of nationalism.

THE CONCILIAR MOVEMENT GROWS

The rupture of the Western Church continued without much hope for a solution. Many tried to reconcile the two factions but nothing ever came of it. Finally a Council was called in Pisa, a city in Northwestern Italy, in 1409. Both reigning Popes of Avignon and Rome were deposed and Alexander V was elected. But the two deposed Popes continued to reign, and thus now there were three reigning Popes. This condition lasted for a decade.

COUNCIL OF BASEL 1431

Pope Martin V called another Council in Basel, a Swiss city, in 1431; but he died before it began. His successor, Eugene IV, wanted to dissolve the Council because it might become too powerful and papal authority might diminish. But the Council representatives persisted and demanded the Pope either come in person or send a representative. The Coucil of Basel had the opportunity of furthering the conciliar movement in the West; but unfortunately the interest dissipated, and the moment was lost. This is a historical fact little known in the West.

CONCLUSION

The Christian West had the grand opportunity of furthering the conciliar movement which in essence said that the delegate bishops would debate, discuss and conclude with mandates ratified by the Church at large. In other words, each local area would send a representative bishop to the Council for the purpose of discussing what was best for the Church. The conciliar movement also espoused the theory that the Council was superior to the Pope and individual bishops. Thus for a fleeting moment in history the Christian West returned to the ancient tradition of the Ecumenical Councils. The conciliar movement was not defeated by papal authority nor by political intervention, but simply forfeited because the West did not pursue it, nor pepetuate it, nor follow it up!

CHAPTER EIGHTEEN

GROWTH OF NATIONAL ORTHODOX CHURCHES

Most modern Western history books on religion and church history generally give the impression that Byzantine Christianity, in contrast with Latin Christianity, was in a period of lifeless decadence during the period between 950 and 1350. This is far from the truth! The conversions to the North of Byzantium, which began in 950, continued to spread geographically. New National Churches joined the Orthodox East through this period of time. While they looked towards Constantinople and its Patriarch as central head, it was not in the juridical and pontifical sense of Rome.

Sometimes the National Churches evolved in a normal way, while other times they emerged as a result of their national leaders wishing to break from the Byzantine Empire. Regardless of the reasons, these National Churches were founded as a result of Byzantine Missionaries, who were inspired and influenced by Sts. Cyril and Methodius. A brief review of some of the past chapters will help in order to pick up the timetable after the Great Schism of 1054. During this period of time, three primary National Orthodox Churches emerged: Bulgarian, Russian and Serbian. The National Orthodox Churches of Greece, Romania, Georgia, Albania, Czechoslovakia, Finland, Japan and others did not emerge until later centuries.

BULGARIAN CHURCH

The Bulgars were a mixture of Southern Slavs and a tribe of Hunnic origin. They settled between the Danube River and the Black Sea in the ninth century. Bulgaria was greatly influenced by Byzantine civilization through the merchants who established trade routes. Although the Bulgarians had been influenced by sporadic contacts with successors of Sts. Cyril and Methodius, their systematic conversion took place under King Boris (852-888). Boris wanted to break with the Byzantine Empire and thought by requesting an Independent Orthodox Church he would bring this about. His vision was finally realized in the middle thirteenth century when Bulgaria became the first Independent National Church of the Slavs.

The Bulgarians, like the Serbians and the Russians, used the Slavonic alphabet and language invented for them by Sts. Cyril and Methodius. Slavonic became the liturgical language as well as the written language of their theological literature. However, their translations were from the Greek and followed the Eastern Orthodox theology. At first Byzantine art and iconography reflected the influence of Constantinople but then evolved into a Byzantine-Slavic style. The purely Slavic style of art and iconography emerged in Russia.

The Bulgarian Church was greatly troubled in the twelfth and thirteenth centuries when a religious movement called *Bogomilism* emerged. The Bogomils (Friends of God) resembled some of the early Christian heresies. Two Gods existed: The good God created Heaven, and the evil God created the world and the Jewish religion of the Old Testament. While they accepted the New Testament, they rejected the miracles of Christ. Eventually the Bogomils were declared heretics and vanished.

In 1235, the Byzantine Emperor recognized Bulgaria as a monarchy; and the Patriarchs of Constantinople, Antioch, Jerusalem and Alexandria granted Patriarchal rank to the Bishop of Sophia and all Bulgaria. Thus Bulgaria became a National Independent Orthodox Church. The Turks invaded Bulgaria in the fifteenth century and brought the nation under total subjugation. However, the Turks permitted the Bulgarians to continue practicing their Orthodox Faith, even though under limited restrictions.

SERBIAN CHURCH

Like Bulgaria, Christianity was first introduced to Serbia in the ninth century through the influence of Sts. Cyril and Methodius. For the most part, the Serbs were influenced by Constantinople. Serbian territory was divided into many independent districts. The northern region was called Croatia or Dalmatia, and the southern region was called Serbia. In 1076 Pope Gregory VII Hildebrand conferred royal dignity upon one of the Croatian chieftains. He also declared a Bishop of Croatia. As a result, the Croatians of northern Serbia became Roman Catholic. Even though attempts were made many times to convert them, the Serbs in the southern region remained Orthodox.

In the second half of the twelfth century the southern region consolidated into a kingdom under Stephen Nemanja who became the first Serbian Emperor. Stephen had two sons, Stephan and Rastko. Rastko became a monk and took the name of Sabba. In 1195 Stephen relinquished the throne to his older son, Stephan, and became a monk. He took the name of Simeon. With his younger son, Sabba, Simeon founded the Studenitsa Serbian Monastery on Mount Athos, where many church leaders of the Serbian Church were trained. Simeon died in 1200. Stephan, however,
did not prove to be a very good leader. Civil disorder broke out, and Stephan negotiated with Pope Innocent III with the promise to bring Serbia under Rome if the Pope would help. This was the time that the Latins dominated Constantinople and some parts of the Balkan peninsula. The people asked Sabba, who was still of the royal family, to return to Serbia and help them avoid subservience to the Pope. Sabba returned to Serbia in 1208 and calmed their fears. He also convinced his brother to renounce his action, which Stephan did.

Sabba went to Nicaea, the temporary capital of the Byzantine Empire [Recall the Fourth Crusade captured Constantinople], requested and obtained from the Byzantine Emperor and Ecumenical Patriarch recognition of an Independent Serbian Orthodox Church. Sabba was consecrated Archbishop to head the new National Serbian Orthodox Church. Sabba was proclaimed a Saint by the Serbian Orthodox Church because he used his faith in the

Orthodox Church to settle both the political and religious strife. Clearly St. Sabba (1174-1237) shaped Serbian Orthodox Christianity. He died on January 4, 1237.

RUSSIAN CHURCH

It was in Russia that Eastern Orthodox Christianity made its most extensive contribution and gains. Russians were first exposed to Christianity when Varangians became mercenaries for the Byzantine armies and the commercial caravan trade routes extended along the Dnieper River. Christianity finally came to Kievan Russia when Vladimir I was converted in 988. Vladimir chose Eastern Orthodoxy over Roman Catholicism. The Russian Church continued to develop and grow through the next two centuries.

In 1206, Temuchin, or Genghis Khan as he is better known, became ruler of the Tatars, a fierce Mongolian tribe of Eastern Asia. Genghis Khan conquered the Chinese Empire and then turned to the west, reaching the Russian border in 1223. However, the Mongolians did not conquer Russia until 1240. Russia remained under Mongol rule for two hundred and forty years. The Mongols permitted the Russians to function politically and socially providing they paid their taxes and did not try to overthrow their rulers. They also permitted the Russian Orthodox Church to continue because Mongol religious laws preached toleration of all religions. The Russian Church helped create and sustain a spirit of national unity.

Novgorod, a city north of Moscow, was threatened by the Crusading Templar Knights from the west and the Mongol army from the east. The Templar Knights from the west wanted to convert Novgorod to Roman Catholicism. The Mongols from the east wanted to devastate Novgorod. Alexander, the Prince of Novgorod, won a remarkable victory at the Neva River. Alexander took on the surname of Nevsky. Alexander then traveled to the foothills of the Tibetan Mountains to meet the Great Khan Batyi who by the middle of the thirteenth century ruled China, India,

Arabia, the Near East and Southern Europe. The Great Khan was so impressed with Alexander Nevsky that he granted him the title of Great Prince of All Russia. The Khan also made a solemn promise that as long as the Russians paid their taxes and obeyed the Tatar laws there would be no more bloodshed. The Russian Orthodox Church proclaimed Alexander Nevsky a saint for willing to sacrifice his life to safeguard the Russian Orthodox Church and the Russian Nation. Tatar rule officially came to an end in 1480 under Ivan III, the Great (1462-1505). By this time Moscow replaced Kiev as the center of the Russian Nation and the head of the Russian Orthodox Church.

Although the Russian Church was practically independent and was certainly a National Church in every sense of the word, she did not receive formal independence until 1589, when the Ecumenical Patriarchate elevated the Metropolitan Archbishop of Moscow to Patriarch. The Russian Orthodox Church continued to grow and contribute to the world right up to the Bolshevik Revolution of 1917. The Russian Orthodox Church continues to be a Living Church today. However, this will be discussed in a later chapter.

REVIEW

Chapters Thirteen through Eighteen brought us from the eleventh century through the fourteenth century. We saw the development, causes, results and consequences of the Great Schism of 1054. We also saw the attempts at reunion of East and West, which were always predicated on submission to Rome. Next we studied the Periods of Scholasticism and Renaissance Humanism, and the influence they had on the West. This was followed by the Decline of the Papacy and the shortlived Conciliar Movement. Finally, we noted the Growth and Expansion of the National Orthodox Churches. Now we are going to enter the fourth period which includes the Fall of the Byzantine Empire in the East and the Protestant Reformation in the West.

CHAPTER NINETEEN

THE FALL OF CONSTANTINOPLE 1453

Emperor Constantine XI Paleologus (1449-1453) had just returned from the Council of Florence-Ferrara (1439) where he had forced most of the Eastern Bishops to sign a union with the Pope. In return the Pope would send troops and supplies to ward off Muhammed II who had set his sight on claiming Constantinople and all the Byzantine East as part of the Ottoman Empire. So opposed to Papal subjugation were the Byzantine Greeks that they cried out, *"Better to fall under the Sultan's sword than the Pope's sandal!"* Muhammed, or Mehmet, as he was called in Turkish, had been educated by Byzantine Greeks and knew well the theological controversy between East and West. He also knew that this was the time to strike.

PREPARATION

During the latter part of 1452, Muhammed II gathered a huge army and proceeded to plan his strategy. His father Murad II had made a treaty with the Byzantines; therefore, Mehmet had to devise a scheme to rouse dissension and provoke retaliation from them. First he built a castle facing the narrowest point of the Bosporus Straits, thereby cutting off supplies and support from the north. His ships and armies harrassed by destroying and pillaging some coastal churches. The Byzantine Emperor finally protested in early 1453, and Muhammed II found the provocation to openly declare war. Late March the Ottoman armada made its way up the Dardanelles and into the Sea of Marmara. The army assembled in Thrace just above Constantinople. His greatest weapon, however, was a huge cannon manufactured specifically for his needs.

Cannons had been used in Western European warfare for over one hundred years, but their maximum performance was limited to dispersing enemy troops in the field. Even though the walls of Constantinople were well over one thousand years old, and although they had been weakened badly during the Crusades, still the European cannons were no match for them. Mehmet engaged the services of an Hungarian engineer named Urban who built a huge cannon for him which measured twenty-six feet in barrel length and eight inches in diameter. The cannon had to be drawn by sixty oxen and serviced by two hundred men. Urban also built smaller yet powerful cannons which could be used by both the artillery and the naval battle ships.

REACTION OF THE GREEKS

Immediately after the declaration of war, Constantine set to work to put the city in a state of defense. The Emperor had thirty fighting ships in his harbor and in the Golden Horn, plus some eight thousand soldiers. However, there were two advantages: The City formed a triangular peninsula which was surrounded by a five-mile triple wall on the land, a huge wall along the Sea of Marmara and a three-mile lesser wall along the Golden Horn. The Golden Horn was a body of water that separated the City from Pera, the body of land to the northeast. The Golden Horn further enhanced the strength of both the army and the navy because a thick chain was fixed across the mouth at the opening. Thus the Golden Horn served as a haven for the ships, as well as a moat for the city walls. Constantine XI Paleologus employed the military service of a Genoese general named John Justiani Longo.

THE SIEGE BEGINS

April 2, 1453, the day after Easter Sunday for the Orthodox Greeks, Muhammed II assembled his entire army outside the land walls, where he set up headquarters. Before he began, he sent a message to the Emperor demanding a voluntary surrender. In return the Greeks were promised that the citizens and their belongings would be spared, according to the Koran. If they refused the offer, they would be shown no mercy. The Emperor and his citizens had little faith in the promise and refused. Thus on Friday, April 6th, Muhammed II gave his order and the cannons began their heavy bombardment of the walls. They continued to attack unrelentlessly; on April 11th Urban's huge cannon began to bombard. While the land army, was bombarding the walls the Turkish fleet was also ordered to enter the battle from the Black Sea.

The Muslim ships soon commanded the waterways and cut the Byzantines off from outside supplies. But Mehmet still could not proceed into the city, either by land or water. Once again he turned to his engineers for a solution.

A BOLD PLAN

Muhammed II realized he could not penetrate the land walls no matter how ceaselessly he bombarded them. With his engineers he devised a plan to render the Golden Horn waterway powerless, both as a haven and a moat. With this plan he would force the Emperor and his general to redistribute their troops in order to protect the Golden Horn side. Thus vulnerable points in the walls would present themselves.

A few miles northeast of the Golden horn Mehmet had cradles lowered into the water and the ships tied on to them. Then he had pulleys drag them up on the shore and across the narrow strip of land by teams of oxen and thousands of men. At the same time he had a large army cross a pontoon bridge at a point where the Golden Horn narrows considerably. In this manner Mehmet forced the Byzantines to redistribute their defending troops and weakened all the walls. In spite of the bold plan, Muhammed was still unable to penetrate the city.

THE END APPROACHES

By the end of May 1453, afer eight weeks of constant

battering with cannons, the Greeks were still able to hold off the enemy. Unless provisions, supplies and food were sent soon from outside, the soldiers and citizens would be starved into surrender. Nevertheless, Muhammed II decided to make one more assault on the City. If he failed, he would take it as an omen that the City was not to be his. He increased the bombardment intensely for two more days. On Monday, May 28th, he ordered all fighting to stop and declared it a day of rest and atonement that his warriors might be prepared for the final assault on Tuesday, May 29th.

Shortly after midnight, Muhammed summoned his troops and ordered them to the ready position. First he sent in his irregulars, the troops made up of malcontents, dissidents and mercenaries. After two hours of futile fighting, the Sultan ordered them to retreat. Next Mehmet sent in his regular army troops by the thousands, along with the artillery and the cannons. By dawn they too were pulled away by the Sultan. Still the Greeks defended their walls with bravery and heroism, aborting any major catastrophe. By this time, of course, they were near exhaustion.

It was left to the Sultan's privileged and favored corps to complete the third and final phase of the assault --the famous Janissaries. Every Janissary at this time was of Christian origin but had been brought up from childhood to be a devout Muslim, to regard his Janissary regiment as his family, and the Sultan as his commander and father. Line after line of fresh, fanatically disciplined soldiers rushed up to the walls. Still the Byzantine Greeks held their ground and might possibly have endured the charge had not a misfortune befallen them. General John Justiniani Longo was seriously wounded. As word was passed from post to post, panic began to strike; and the soldiers left their posts. Seeing this, Mehmet personally led his Janissaries and all the other troops for one final attack. Constantine XI Paleologus and many others were killed. The battle was over for both the City and the Empire.

THREE DAY PILLAGE AND SACK

Muhammed II gave his soldiers three days to pillage, sack and loot. At the end of the three days they were to leave the City. The troops swept through the City like a violent flood, slaying everyone they met in the streets --men, women and children, without discrimination. They ripped off jewels, gems, stones, gold and silver from icons, books, religious articles and altars. They burned and desecrated churches, buildings, houses, hospitals, schools and the harbors. Monasteries and convents were plundered. Once the three-day period ended, Muhammed II entered the City and declared martial law. It is said he had tears in his eyes when he saw that more damage had been done by the looters than by the constant fifty-two days of bombardment by his cannons. Nevertheless, he rebuilt the City and made it the capital of his empire. Muhammed II died in 1481.

THE ORTHODOX CHURCH UNDER THE TURKISH YOKE

Muhammed II formed a self-governing community for all Orthodox Christians within his empire. He placed them under the authority of the Ecumenical Patriarch, who would be responsible to the Sultan. A Synod of Bishops was formed to assist him in his administrative duties. Together, Patriarch and Synod, they were empowered to hear all religious and civil cases involving Orthodox Christians. Only criminal cases and cases in which a Muslim was involved went to the Turkish courts. The Christians could worship freely but could not bear arms. The taking of young male children to form the corps of Janissaries was to continue unopposed. These were the conditions handed to the Orthodox Church under the Ottoman Empire, which lasted until the Greek Revolution of 1821, through the turn of the twentieth century. The Ottoman Empire lasted until 1923, when under the leadership of Kemal Mustafa Ataturk, Turkey became a Modern State.

CONCLUSION

The purpose of this chapter is not to instill hatred nor animosity but to illustrate what the Greeks in the City of Constantinople had to contend with, endured and suffered —at the same time, to show their courage and heroic bravery and the odds against which they fought. Nevertheless, all of Eastern Christendom, with the exception of Russia, fell under the Turkish Yoke, or an "Iron Curtain," if you will.

The Ottoman subjugation of the Orthodox East lasted from the fifteenth through the nineteenth centuries. It was during these years that the early settlers and those who followed them came to America. It is also clear why those who came to America were Protestants and Roman Catholics, and not Orthodox. The Orthodox who were under the Turkish Yoke were unable to come to America. Russia alone was free during this span and sent missionaries to Alaska and the Aleutian Islands once they were claimed as Russian Territories. Nevertheless, the Orthodox East remained strong during this four hundred years of tyranny and bondage. It was the Orthodox Church that perpetuated both the faith and the spirit of liberation, which ultimately came in the nineteenth century. Once the Orthodox Christians in the Balkan, Slavic and Middle Eastern Countries were liberated, they too, came to the New World. But before we discuss them, we will focus our attention on Western Europe and what took place there during the fourteenth through sixteenth century. We will study the Protestant Reformation and its spread throughout Western Europe and America.

CHAPTER TWENTY

BEFORE THE PROTESTANT REFORMATION

The Protestant Reformation encompasses one third of the History of the Christian Church. The Country we live in is predominantly a Protestant-oriented Nation. Protestant Churches are found throughout all the cities and rural areas. You know who Roman Catholics are because you have read about them. But who are the Lutherans, Presbyterians, Episcopalians, Methodists, Baptists, United Church of Christ and a multitude of other Churches who are neither Orthodox nor Roman Catholic? Where did they stem from? What are their basic teachings? How do they differ from Roman Catholics and Orthodox? What happened to cause these Churches to break away from Roman Catholicism and create new Churches?

Recall the *"Babylonian Captivity"* when there were two and three Popes in Rome and Avignon, France. The Papacy suffered a decline in power, authority and prestige. By this time the Church of Rome had accumulated much territory, was involved in the Feudal System and conducted battle campaigns which required large treasuries to sustain them. Popes regarded themselves as having the prerogative and privilege of extracting regular and extraordinary taxes from all the Christian Provinces of the West for the Papal Treasury. The Popes also influenced the assignments and appointments of government offices, and land ownership titles. It is very important to bear these points in mind, because, although they were not necessarily the reasons that precipitated the Protestant Reformation, they gave the reformers the cause to stand up and be heard. Another important point is that these early reformers, unlike their predecessors, had the support of both rulers and the masses. Two such individuals were John Wyclif and John Huss.

JOHN WYCLIF (1320-1384)

John Wyclif disputed the religious authority of Rome to intervene in English government and to demand tax assessments. He advised Parliament not to pay. He disputed the Papal System, the hierarchal structure of the Church and the teaching on Transubstantiation. The reader will recall that Scholasticism attempted to explain in detail how the bread and wine become the Body and Blood of Christ in the Liturgy through the use of philosophical concepts and terms. The outer appearance, they said, remained material substance while the inner, unseen part of the bread and wine changed into a spiritual substance. This is called **Transubstantiation. The Orthodox Church simply accepted that outwardly the Gifts still appear as bread and wine, but inwardly, in some mysterious, miraculous and inexplicable manner, they become the Body and Blood of Jesus Christ. Jesus said, "this is My Body....this is My Blood."** (Matthew 26:26-28) **The Orthodox Church does not attempt to explain how this change takes place, but rather accepts it as a mystery.**

Wyclif also disputed the doctrine of salvation as taught by Rome. He questioned whether a person could be saved by doing good and meritorious works, even for the good of mankind and the Church. He was one of the first of the long line of reformers to emphasize the Bible and deemphasize Holy Tradition. Wyclif's greatest contribution was to translate great portions of the Bible from Latin into English. This, too, was met with great opposition because it was unthinkable for any but the clergy to read the Bible at that time. Wyclif died in 1384 without having his teachings leave too much of an impression in England. But they did spread to Bohemia (Czechoslovakia) and later over into Germany. John Wyclif was one of the forerunners of the Protestant Reformation, even though he lived two centuries before it.

JOHN HUSS (1369-1415)

John Huss was a professor of Philosophy at the University of Prague, Bohemia (Czechoslovakia). Scandalized by the immorality of his time and influenced by the writings of Wyclif, Huss reacted vehementaly when papal representatives came to Bohemia to sell **indulgences.** [Indulgences are discussed in the next paragraph.] Since Wyclif's writings were declared heretical by the Council of Constance (1414-1418), and Huss was a follower of Wyclif, he was imprisoned and tried as a heretic. John Huss was burned at the stake on July 6, 1415.

This practice set the unfortunate precedent of what later came to be called the Inquisition in the West. Inquisitors were appointed and sent by the Church of Rome to inquire into the views and teachings of individuals suspected of heresy. If found guilty, the tribunal could mete out punishment. If the suspects refused to recant, the inquisitors had the authority to torture them, excommunicate them, and, in some instances, put them to death for their heresy.

PENANCES-TREASURY OF MERITS-INDULGENCES

In the Early Church certain disciplinary methods called penances were imposed upon sinners, depending upon the seriousness of the sins. As a general rule, they were required to perform certain penances: prayers, charitable works,etc. Sometimes the sinners were prohibited from receiving Holy Communion for a period of time. But with repentance, confession and the fulfillment of penances set forth, the sinners were restored to full grace in the life of the Church.

By the Period of Scholasticism, the Western Church gave penances a different meaning and a different purpose. The penances were used as a method of soliciting funds and increasing the Papal treasury, which was constantly in need to take care of all the lands and armies of the papacy. By the thirteenth century, Western theology introduced a method of acquiring money for the Papal treasury through what was called the **Treasury of Merits.** To understand how this system worked it is necessary to go into some theological background.

Jesus died on the Cross; this sacrifice more than gave satisfaction for it satisfied Adam's sentence of death and alienation from God's heavenly kingdom. The outpouring of Jesus' Blood on the Cross more than compensated for the grace needed to save mankind. Therefore, there was a **surplus of grace** deposited in a reservoir, storehouse (thus theorized Scholasticism). In addition, they added, the Martyrs and Saints who gave up their lives proffered a **superabundance of grace** which was added to Christ's **surplus grace.** This reservoir, or storehouse of excess grace came to be called the **Treasury of Merits** (Bank Account of superabundance grace) in Roman Catholic theology.

> **The Orthodox Church merely states that dogmatically we believe Jesus' death sacrifice on the Cross satisfied Adam's death sentence. The outpouring of Jesus' Blood on the Cross reconciled and united mankind to God's heavenly kingdom. Since man still had the capacity to sin again, Christ founded the Church through which man could remain in God's grace. Penance and good works have nothing to do with merits, superabundance grace and purgatory.**

The Treasury of Merits was further supported and reinforced with the Papal theory of the **Petrine Promise** and the **Papal Vicarship** of each subsequent Bishop of Rome. If St. Peter was indeed Christ's Vicar and the dispenser of the surplus grace in the Treasury of Merits, then it follows that each subsequent heir to the papal throne becomes the guardian and dispenser of grace in the Treasury of Merits. How is this applied in practice?

The Popes utilized the penitential disciplinary practice of the Early Church as a basis for soliciting funds. The Western Christians were given to believe that their charitable act, along with repentance, brought about a forgiveness of sins through the authority invested in the Pope by Christ. It was determined that the sins would be forgiven later in a place called **Purgatory.** Purgatory, Roman Catholic theology claims, is an intermediary period between death and final judgment. According to this fabricated teaching, after death the souls of sinners pass through a cleansing by fire; the length of time is determined by the seriousness of the sin. The penances were certified with a paper called **indulgence**, which mitigated punishment and lessened the time spent in Purgatory. The authority for issuance was the Treasury of Merits.

> **The Orthodox Church has no such teaching as Purgatory. Orthodox theology teaches there is an Intermediary Stage between death and final judgment. However it is not a stage of cleansing; rather it is a period of partial judgment. That is to say, those who lived the type of life on earth that God would want, begin partaking of God's heavenly kingdom partially. Conversely, those who did not, begin partaking of the loneliness and alienation from God's grace partially. In Orthodox theology the time for repentance and forgiveness is in this life.**

Sometime after the eleventh century, Indulgences replaced the penitential discipline of the Early Church in the West. The Crusaders, for example, were granted Indulgences in appreciation for their attempts to liberate the Holy Lands. By the fourteenth and fifteenth centuries the sale of Indulgences became widespread. As we shall see in the next chapter, the sale of Indulgences will become the springboard for the Protestant Reformation. Indulgences, Treasury of Merits, and Purgatory first came under attack by John Huss. However, it will be Martin Luther, the Augustinian monk and professor of the famous German University of Wittenburg who will be the catalyst for the Protestant Reformation. We will meet him in the next chapter.

CONCLUSION

It is important for the objective reader of church history to understand that the Protestant Reformation did not just happen by chance. To the contrary, The Reformation was the end result of many circumstances and conditions which had been developing in Western Europe over several centuries. We must bear in mind the following:

-Nationalism arose with the emergence of New States.
-The indigenous languages, national literature and customs, along with the opening of local universities created a self-awareness and self-consciousness.
-Commerce and industry provided the foundation for capitalism.

-The leaders of the Western Church became all the more immersed in the wealth and materialism of the world.

The above, --the Emergence of New States, Universities, Scholasticism, Humanism and Capitalism, along with the decline of the Papacy, all laid the groundwork and planted the seeds for the Protestant Reformation which took place in 1517 A.D., as we shall see in the next chapter.

CHAPTER TWENTY-ONE

THE PROTESTANT REFORMATION

MARTIN LUTHER

INTRODUCTION

Before studying Martin Luther and the Protestant Reformation, it is necessary to discuss the one person who perhaps had the most profound influence upon Luther: Desiderius Erasmus. Erasmus, a Dutch Christian Humanist and Greek scholar, spent almost a decade (1505-1514) collecting ancient Greek manuscripts of the New Testament and correcting the Latin texts. In March of 1516 Erasmus printed the New Testament in Greek. This was the first copy to reach the public. It had an introduction, a commentary and a new Latin translation. By the following August a copy had reached Martin Luther, one of the youngest members of the faculty of theology at the University of Wittenberg, Germany, who was lecturing on St. Paul's Epistle to the Romans. Six years later Luthur translated the New Testament into German using Erasmus' Greek text as a basis. Although Desiderius Erasmus remained with the Church of Rome, Martin Luther broke away, thus causing the beginning of the Protestant Reformation.

MARTIN LUTHER (1483-1546)

The greatest figure of the Protestant Reformation was Martin Luther, born in Eisleben, Germany, November 10, 1483. At age twenty-five, and as an Augustinian monk, he received his Doctorate in Theology and was appointed professor of Philosophy at Wittenberg by Frederick the Wise, the Great Elector of Saxony. By 1517 Martin Luther was regarded as an authority on Holy Scripture.

By 1513 Pope Leo X had put the Papacy in great debt. He also wanted funds to build St. Peter's Church in Rome.

Therefore he sent out Archbishops, Bishops and Monks to solicit funds through the sale of Indulgences. Archbishop Albert of Mainz, in whose Diocese Wittenberg lay, gave Tetzel, a Dominican Monk, permission to sell Indulgences there. When Martin Luther opposed the practice and sale of Indulgences, at first it appeared to be a squabble between two Monastic Orders. However, as we shall see, there was much more to it.

As was the practice at that time, when announcements were made, they were attached to the front door of the Church. In a document called **Ninety-Five Theses,** which Luther nailed to the announcement board on the church door, he listed his opposition to the sale of Indulgences. Thus he also questioned the authority of Rome to issue Indulgences. This, in turn, brought into question Papal Authority, Infallibility and the authority of the Councils over Scripture.

ENCOUNTER WITH THE PAPACY

Had Luther been someone else or lived in a different region during a different time, he might possibly have been silenced. But he was not. Luther also protested against forcing Germans to pay for the construction of St. Peter's Church in Rome. Thus when Luther opposed Rome's errors in theology, Frederick the Wise, the faculty of Wittenberg, and the masses all supported him. He said the Indulgences did not remove the guilt of sin, the Pope could not exercise jurisdiction in Purgatory, and the saints did not accumulate surplus grace credits.

Once Pope Leo X realized Luther was serious, he ordered him to recant. He sent Cardinal Cajetan to debate with him in Augsburg, a German city near Wittenberg, on October 11, 1518. This was a significant concession because the Pope unwittingly placed the scene of controversy and action in Luther's home territory. Luther refused to recant and proceeded to attack the doctrinal foundation and claim to Papal Infallibility. This led to a second meeting at Leipzig in July 17, 1519, in which John

Eck of Ingolstadt debated with Luther. Eck maneuvered Luther into declaring the Council of Constance as having unjustly declared Huss a heretic and that neither Pope nor Ecumenical Councils were infallible.

Thus Martin Luther, without intending to, made a break from the Church of Rome. He began writing and publishing tracts and pamphlets against Rome, against Holy Tradition and the Ecumenical Councils, which he thought supported Papal claims. Slowly his theology turned from the traditional teachings commonly accepted in the Early Christian Church to a theology which selected those found only in the Holy Bible. For example, he accepted Baptism and Eucharist as valid Sacraments because they were mentioned specifically in the Bible. Since Indulgences and Penances were predicated on *"good works,"* Luther declared that man can be saved only through faith. Thus the traditional teaching of the Church --that faith and good works go hand in hand-- was omitted from Luther's theology. Martin Luther opened the door for his contemporaries and successors to pick and choose what they judged to be valid and true, irrespective of the criteria of fifteen centuries of a Living Church.

MARTIN LUTHER EXCOMMUNICATED

On June 15, 1520, Rome issued the Bull of Excommunication condemning Luther and his heretical teachings. Luther wrote a new German translation of the Bible. He urged the dissolution of all monasteries and nunneries, and expressed his approval of marriage of priests, monks and nuns. German princes welcomed the opportunity to seize church lands, and German bankers were happy to see the stop of money flowing to Rome. Luther organized a Reformed Church, The Lutheran Church, and within a generation it became the State Church of half of Germany.

In 1529 the German Churches still in communion with Rome held a meeting at Speyer and drew up an order to outlaw Lutheranism. The Lutheran princes who protested against Rome came to be known as the **"Protestants."** In 1555 a meeting was held in Augsburg at which a settlement was reached whereby each could worship freely. This settlement was called the Peace of Augsburg.

Lutheranism spread northward to Scandinavia, Denmark, Sweden and Central Europe. The Reform Movement did not stop after Martin Luther's death in 1546 but continued through John Calvin and others. The Church of Rome, too, underwent reform as a result of the Counter-Reformation Council of Trent in 1545. John Calvin and the Council of Trent will be discussed in the next chapter.

SUMMARY OF MARTIN LUTHER'S TEACHINGS

Luther insisted that Holy Scripture should be read and interpreted by the individual, and that he should not be inhibited and hampered by other interpreters. He contended that Papal claims and false teachings resulted because of interpretations based on Holy Tradition.

> **The Orthodox Church has always insisted each individual read Holy Scripture, but with the criteria and backdrop of the Apostolic, Post-Apostolic and Patristic Fathers who both lived and passed on the teachings of Christ. In other words, through the Church.**

Luther dispensed with the Fathers and replaced them with man's individual comprehension. However, Luther was later forced to go to the Fathers himself in order to subtantiate his own doctrinal teachings against those who disagreed with him.

In addition to limiting the Sacraments to Baptism, Eucharist and Absolution [Repentance] (thus omitting the other Sacraments), Luther also altered the doctrine of how sinful man is saved. He interpreted Romans 1:17, **"man is saved by faith,"** as "Man is saved by justification of faith alone." [Luther added the word "alone," which is not in the scriptural text.] According to Martin Luther man can receive faith only through God's grace. Even faith is a gift from God. Human nature has radically fallen. Man is totally depraved. Man fell radically under the bondage of sin and death. His entire nature was corrupted. He is utterly incapable of doing anything to remedy his condition.

Luther, along with St. Augustine of the sixth century, believed that when Adam and Eve sinned and fell away from God's grace, they became spiritually dead. As a result of this spiritual death, they could never, again have the will nor the initiative to participate in their own salvation. With Jesus' Coming, God gave mankind the opportunity to be saved ---strictly as a gift from God, without man's participation in any way. Thus, there was no need for good works. This was something fabricated by the Papacy in order to advance and support it. But Luther's one big problem, and one he never resolved, was James 2:17: ***"So, faith by itself, if it has no good works, is dead."***

As was stated in previous chapters, the Orthodox Church, too, disputes Papal Authority, Indulgences, Treasure of Merits and Purgatory. As regards faith and good works, and grace and free will, Orthodox theology also teaches that man is saved by faith and by the grace of God. However, the Patristic Fathers do not agree with St.Augustine and Luther that Adam and Eve died a total spiritual death at their fall. They and their descendents still had will power and the initiative to be saved, but as they fell they sinned more. The more they sinned, the more they fell away from God. Eventually their alienation was so great that God deemed it necessary to come in the Person of Jesus Christ and help them back. With Baptism, a rebirth, a regeneration took place which restored God's grace. The Gift of the Holy Spirit at Baptism, in the Sacraments, in all liturgical services and through faith, fused with man's free will and initiative enables him

to follow God's commandments and be saved. Orthodox theology teaches that two energies are needed for man's salvation: God's grace and man's will.

The immediate problem with Luther's ***"Justification by faith alone"*** is found in the formation of a notion of pre-destination. That is to say, if man has no say-so in his salvation, then God picks and chooses whom He will save and whom He will condemn without any regard to what man is, how he thinks, how he acts and how he lives. Luther, of course, did not declare a doctrine of pre-destination, but his successors did, as we shall see in the next chapter.

CONCLUSION

Once Martin Luther began selecting only those teachings and practices found in the Bible, he opened the door to his contemporaries, followers and successors to pick and choose only those Doctrines, Traditions, Sacraments and Liturgical Services which they judged to be true and valid. The Sacraments (with the exception of Baptism and Eucharist), Monasticism, Priesthood, Holy Tradition and many of the basic doctrines were dropped by the Protestant Reformers as a result of Martin Luther's break with Rome. The next three chapters will illustrate how one break in the sixteenth century brought about over two hundred fifty Protestant Denominations in America.

CHAPTER TWENTY-TWO

THE REFORMATION CONTINUES

JOHN CALVIN

INTRODUCTION

While the German Reformation was taking place, other reform movements were concurrently happening in other parts of Europe. One place was Switzerland. Two reformers emerged from Switzerland, a German Swiss named Hudreich Zwingli and Frenchman named John Calvin. The latter we will hear about shortly.

Huldreich Zwingli (1484-1531), a priest, first came into conflict with the Church of Rome over the sale of Indulgences. While Zwingli agreed with Luther against monastic vows, clerical celibacy, treasury of merits, purgatory and good works, he made a further departure in the Eucharist. Luther believed that the actual presence of Jesus Christ was to be found in the consecrated elements. Zwingli regarded the Eucharist to be primarily a Memorial Supper through which the worshippers were bound together in an expression of loyalty to their Lord. To Zwingli, Luther's view seemed to be an irrational persistence of Roman Catholic superstition. Zwingli died October 11, 1531, during an uprising between Swiss Protestants and Roman Catholics. The reform movement spread throughout Switzerland and eventually made its way to Geneva, the French Swiss center, where another Protestant giant emerged in the person of John Calvin.

JOHN CALVIN (1509-1564)

John Calvin was born in Paris July 10, 1509. Unlike most reformers, Calvin never entered the priesthood. In 1535, at the age of twenty-six, John Calvin wrote and published what was probably the most influential book of the Protestant Reformation, *The Institutes of the Christian*

Religion. John Calvin organized **The Reformed Church** according to his doctrines and their interpretation.

CALVIN'S INSTITUTES

Calvin's Institutes, as his book of doctrine came to be known, presented a clear and concise catechism on the Christian Faith held by the Protestant Reformers. The teachings reflected Calvin's philosophical interpretation of God, Christianity and Man. Three outstanding points to be found in Calvin's Institutes are as follows:

A. PREDESTINATION

Although both Luther and Zwingli taught predestination, it was not clearly defined until Calvin wrote his Institutes. Calvin based his doctrine of Man on St. Augustine's teachings of the Fall of Adam and Eve. Augustine believed that Adam and Eve, and all generations which followed, had their freedom of will darkened to such a point that all they were capable of ever doing again was to sin. In short, theirs was a spiritual death, total depravity, after the fall.

The Patristic Fathers, whose teaching the Orthodox East espoused, taught that Adam and Eve fell away from God as a result of their alienation from God. Theirs was not a spiritual death nor total depravity. The more they sinned the more they fell away from God, and the less they could communicate with Him. The Orthodox Church never condemned St. Augustine, but rather accepted his teaching as another interpretation because he never carried it any further.

It was John Calvin that took St. Augustine's theory and carried it a step further by declaring that man was capable of only sinning after the Fall, that this was God's will. Out of this extension emerged Calvin's **Doctrine of Unconditional Election,** or Predestination. Since man could do nothing but sin, and it was God's will to allow this, therefore, Calvin believed that God "Elected," (chooses) who is to be saved and who is to be damned.

Calvin also introduced the **Doctrine of Limited Atonement** and the **Doctrine of Irresistable Grace.** In the former, Calvin taught that Jesus did not die for the sins of the whole world, just for the sins of the Elect. The atonement was limited. In the latter Calvin taught that those who were chosen could not reject nor refuse the Election. There is no choice nor free will involved in the process.

Calvin's purpose was to eliminate the Papal teaching of merits and good works, and at the same time, to free man from his worries and concern about himself in order that he might devote all his energy to serving a Sovereign Lord. He said the chief function of man is not to save himself or to be assured that he is saved, but to honor God. In any case, he contended, man is already **"saved"** or **"damned"** by God and no worry will make any difference. Needless to say, these false teachings were contrary to the Patristic teachings of the Christian Church held both in the East and the West.

The Doctrines of Unconditional Election, Limited Atonement and Irresistable Grace run contrary to the Orthodox Christian teaching about man. There is no margin for man's initiative and the exercise of free will to better himself, and achieve his theosis with God. God's gift of salvation through grace is given to us freely. We do nothing to merit it. But the choice is still ours. Thus we receive objective salvation freely. But in order for us to have subjective salvation, we must certainly exercise our God-given gift of free will to accept or reject salvation.

B. A MORAL CODE OF LIFE
BASED ON HOLY SCRIPTURE

Like Zwingli and Luther, Calvin abandoned all sacraments except Baptism and Eucharist. The latter he regarded merely as a symbolic memorial. He stripped the church services of all rites and ceremonies for which he could not find express authority in the Bible. He did away with vestments, holy water fonts, stained glass windows, icons, statues, incense and organ music. He replaced the altar with a single table, eliminated the Crucifix and all Christian symbols. Worship consisted of a simple form of the Eucharist with a sermon.

Calvin taught that the bread and wine became the Body and Blood of Jesus Christ only for the believers. For the non-believers it remained bread and wine. Thus he departed from Luther and the traditional Christian teaching on the Eucharist. Later Calvinists confined the Eucharist to an occasional practice, and replaced it with Scripture reading, preaching of a sermon, psalm singing, the Lord's Prayer and extemporaneous prayers of moment. They frowned on light amusements such as dancing, games and the theatre, and lived a puritan-type life.

C. PRESBYTERIAN CHURCH GOVERNMENT

Calvin called for a more democratic Church government in contrast with the hierarchal structure of the Church of Rome, centered around the Papacy. He did away with monasteries, nunneries, cardinals, archbishops and Bishops, and only kept the **"Presbyters,"** the priests. To them he added lay elders and formed the **"Presbytery,"** which would govern the Church through local assemblies.

Calvin organized the city of Geneva into a City-Church and governed and administered it with his "Presbytery." He set out to create God's Kingdom on earth based on the Institutes. He ruled both the City of Geneva and the Church as an autocratic dictator from 1541 to 1564, when he died. The Presbytery, under Calvin's leadership, imposed church and civil rules upon the citizenry of Geneva. They punished religious dissenters by imprisonment, exile and even death, when they thought the heresy called for it. Thus the Calvinists had their Inquisition Period, too.

CALVINISM SPREADS

Calvinist Protestantism spread throughout the European Continent more rapidly and more effectively than Lutheranism because it was more international in character and far less nationalistic. Although Calvin succeeded in converting Geneva into a City-Church, it did not remain so after his death. While Martin Luther is regarded the Father of the Protestant Reformation, it is Calvinism that influenced the theology of the Reformed Churches which comprise, primarily, the Main-Line Protestant Reformation Churches in Western Europe and America.

GENERAL SURVEY OF PROTESTANTISM

The Protestant Churches at first appearance seem to be churches interested only in the fundamental teachings of the Bible and the Early Christian Church. This observation is not only an oversimplification , but an erroneous one as well. There are several dramatic differences between Calvinist Protestantism and the Early Christian Church, and it is necessary for us to recognize them.

1) CREATION AND FALL OF MAN

The Holy Bible says, ***"Let us make man in our image after our likeness."*** (Genesis 1:26) According to the writings of the Early Christian Fathers, as well as the Great Teachers of the Golden Age, the two words, **"image"** and **"likeness,"** have two different meanings. According to Western theology, especially Lutheranism and Calvanism, they mean one and the same. Protestantism believes that Adam and Eve were created perfect in the absolute sense and that they were given all the knowledge, grace and strength, along with the free will, to do only that which God instructed them to do. This teaching was based on St.Augustine. Therefore, when Adam and Eve fell from God's grace, they lost everything: knowledge, grace, strength and free will.

Orthodox theology, following the teachings of the Early Christian Writers and the Patristic Fathers, teaches that God created Adam and Eve in "His Image," which endowed them with knowledge, grace, strength and free will to carry out His instructions. That is to say, to perfect themselves. Therefore, they were created perfect in the potential sense, not in the absolute sense. The process of perfecting themselves -achieving theosis- would render them God's "likeness" -the state of perfect harmony and fellowship with God.

In other words, Luther, Zwingli and Calvin taught that man was created perfect in an absolute and complete sense, whereas the Church of the Ecumenical Councils taught -and the Eastern Orthodox Church continues to teach- that man was created perfect in a potential sense. The movement from "image" to "likeness" -theosis- is one of development, through God's grace and injunctions, using free will and initiative.

In short, the Orthodox Church holds a somewhat less exalted idea about man's condition before he fell from God's grace than do Protestants. Adam did not fall from a great height of knowledge and perfection, as much as from a state of undeveloped capability. As a result of the fall, man's mind was darkened and his will power was impaired to such a degree that he could no longer hope to achieve God's "likeness" on his own. However, he did retain his freedom of will and choice.

But unlike Calvinism, the Orthodox Church does not teach that man was utterly depraved and totally incapable of good desires and free will. God's "image" in man was distorted but not destroyed. This is the dramatic difference! Calvinism leaves no room for human freedom, something which Orthodox theology cannot accept. Since God had not taken away man's "image," man still had the will to obey Him or disobey Him. Eventually, of course, man's sin took him far away from God —so far away that God decided to become Man in order to save mankind from the course of self-annihilation.

2) THE EUCHARIST

Jesus commanded the Eucharist to be performed throughout the ages as a means of uniting man with Himself mystically. The Eucharist was performed in Apostolic, Early Christian times and throughout the centuries both in the East and West. Although the Church of Rome deviated from the early practice format of the Eucharist, nevertheless, it remained as the central means of worship. In Lutheranism, the purpose of the Eucharist becomes obscured because certain practices were being abused by the Church of Rome.

Two prevailing teachings on the Eucharist emerged: One group of Lutheran theologians taught that the consecrated host of the Eucharist is truly the Body and Blood of Christ. The other group taught that the host is the Body and Blood of Christ only for the believing communicant. Also, those unused consecrated hosts are returned to a tabernacle and consecrated again at a later liturgy. However, today most Lutherans accept the former and reject the latter.

Hudreich Zwingli came to regard the Eucharist as a memorial service through which the worshippers expressed their bond of loyalty to their Lord. Calvin furthered the departure from traditional practice and reserved it as a service to be performed occasionally, replacing it with the typical Protestant service performed today: Scripture, sermon, hymns and prayer.

Luther, Zwingli and Calvin fought against practices and abuses they observed in use by the Church of Rome at the time. The Eucharist had been distorted and the sacraments misused. Indulgences and good works had been used to reinforce the false claims of the Papacy. Papal tyranny left no margin and latitude for expression and openness of theological discussion. All of these abuses, coupled with troubled times, gave the reformers -especially Luther and Calvin- the opportunity to express their grievances and theological differences.

Luther, Zwingli and Calvin may have wished only to reform the Church of Rome; however, in the process they cast out traditional teachings and introduced new ones. Martin Luther broke with Rome, denounced the Papacy, the Ecumenical Councils and the Patristic Fathers. Huldreich Zwingli became radical and removed age-old and time-tested worship practices and teachings of the Church indiscriminately. John Calvin, wanting to create a more democratic Church, became more autocratic than the Popes he accused and opposed, even to the point of ruthlessly putting religious dissenters to death. The Eucharist, from the central core of corporate worship, became a memorial service to be observed occasionally.

Once the guidelines of traditional theology were cast aside, freedom was given to each individual to reform the Church according to his personal interpretation and comprehension. Hence there are some 260 Protestant Denominations in the United States today. Even the Main-Line Protestant Reformation Churches are divided amongst themselves. For example, there are four separate Lutheran Bodies and as many Presbyterian and Baptist Bodies in America today.

In the next chapter we will see the Reformation Movement spreading to England. While the reasons and causes may have differed, nevertheless they forged the formation of the Episcopal Churches. They, in turn, laid the foundation for the emergence of the Methodist, Baptist and Congregational Churches.

CHAPTER TWENTY-THREE

THE ENGLISH REFORMATION

The religious revolt in Germany and Switzerland can truthfully be regarded as a Religious Reformation because that is what the reformers sought to do. But the split that England made with the Church of Rome was not because of dissatisfaction with religious beliefs and practices. Rather, it resulted because of political and personal conflicts between King Henry VIII and the Pope.

HENRY VIII (1507-1547)

King Henry VIII, who was a defender of the Papacy, in 1527 asked Pope Clement VII to annul his seventeen-year marriage to his Spanish wife, Katherine of Aragon. Since the Pope would not annul his marriage, Henry declared the Church of England independent of Rome in 1533 and positioned himself as the Head of the Church of England. The Archbishop of Canterbury annulled his marriage to Katherine, and he married Anne Boleyn. As Head of the Church of England, he issued the Book of Common Prayer in English and replaced the Latin language with English in worship. Henry VIII died in 1547, after a forty year reign.

EDWARD VI (1547-1553)

Henry was succeeded by his ten year old son, Edward VI, son of Jane Seymour, his third wife. Edward's guardian was Archbishop Cranmer of Canterbury, who although he had been influenced by Zwinglian radicalism, did not allow it to show during Henry's reign. Once Edward took the throne, Cranmer introduced a mixture of Protestant Zwinglianism, Lutheranism and Calvanism. Marriage of the clergy was introduced; altars, icons, statues and vestments were removed. A second edition of the Book of Common Prayer was published which was more Calvanist in character than the previous conservative one under

Henry VIII. Finally, in 1552 Cranmer issued the Forty-Two Articles of Religion in which he declared Holy Scripture alone to be the Source of Divine Knowledge; Justification by faith alone in order to be saved; Baptism and Eucharist to be the only two Sacraments; and, Eucharist to be the Body and Blood of Jesus Christ only for the worthy and faithful receiver.

Edward VI died in 1553 and left his half-sister Mary, the daughter of Katherine of Aragon, as the heir to the throne. Mary attempted to restore Roman Catholicism to England. Archbishop Cranmer was put to death along with countless clergy and laity whom she considered a threat. She deposed Bishops who opposed her and excommunicated priests who had married and who had introduced Protestant practices and teachings. Her tyrannical rule won her the title of *Bloody Mary.* She tried to blot out Protestantism in England but only succeeded in curbing it for a while. When she died after only five years of reign, she was succeeded by Elizabeth, the daughter of Anne Boleyn.

QUEEN ELIZABETH (1558-1602)

Elizabeth was not interested in religious reform nor Roman Catholicism. She wanted to restore the power her father had. At first she attempted to pacify both sides with compromises and concessions. But then she took actions which were to have longlasting effect on the Church of England. First she had Parliament pass the Supremacy Act which restored her position as Head of the Church of England. Next was the Uniformity Act which required all the clergy and laity of England to accept the second edition of the Book of Common Prayer. Then, the most consequential was to have the Forty-Two Articles of Faith revised to Thirty-Nine Articles, which she declared to be the true Doctrines of the Church of England.

The Thirty-Nine Articles are synopsized as follows:

a) Holy Tradition is rejected as well as the following Books of the Old Testament: Tobit, Judith, Wisdom of Sirach, Wisdom of Solomon, First Ezra, Baruch, Epistle of Jeremiah and the Three Books of Maccabees. **The Orthodox Church and the Roman Catholic Church regard these books as canonical, but not having equal dogmatic significance as the other Old Testament Books. Therefore, our Old Testament has forty-nine Books while the Protestant Old Testament has only thirty-nine.**

b) Papal authority is rejected. The Monarch of England is simultaneously the Head of the Church. Church law is invalid without the approval of the Monarch and Parliament.

c) Baptism and Eucharist are the only two Sacraments and the latter is to be regarded with the Calvinist interpretation.

d) Purgatory, veneration of icons, statues, Saints, relics and religious symbols are rejected.

e) Calvinist Predestination is rejected, although Justification by faith alone is retained.

f) Only Bishops are recognized as an Order of the Priesthood and successors of the Holy Apostles; priests are just ministers and preachers. (Anglicans are later called Episcopalians, from the Greek word, *Episkopos*, Bishop.)

g) The symbols of ritual such as the Crucifix, vestments, incense, altars, etc., are allowed to remain. (However, the Church of England will divide into High, Broad and Low Church, and the latter two will reject even these.)

Elizabeth was officially excommunicated by Pope Pius V in February of 1570, but she reigned as Queen of England for another thirty-two years. From the English Church sprang several Protestant Churches, which will be discussed in the next chapter.

NON-CONFORMISTS: CONGREGATIONAL CHURCH

Those who did not accept the Uniformity Act (Book of Common Prayer, Episcopal authority, etc.) were called Non-Conformists. They believed each local church should be completely independent, regardless of its size. They contended that Jesus Christ was the Head of the Church. Therefore, Bishops and clergymen were unnecessary. The congregation of believers in the local church were the ones to interpret Scripture and determine their own way of life. The Non-Conformists were organized by Robert Browne and were called the **Congregational Church.** The Congregationalists fled to Holland because they were persecuted in England. Eventually they came to America because their children began learning the language and traditions of Holland.

The Congregationalists arrived in America November 1620. In 1636 they founded Harvard College in Cambridge. They played a major role in the American Revolutionary War. Soon afterward they came into conflict amongst themselves and divided into two Bodies: The one group remained rigid Calvinist and believed in the Holy Trinity while the other group rejected the doctrine of the Holy Trinity and came to be known as **Unitarians.** Two decades ago the **Congregational Church** merged with the **Disciples of Christ Church** and formed the present day **United Church of Christ.**

PROTESTANT EPISCOPAL CHURCH

The Congregationalists and Presbyterians settled in the New England Colonies while the Anglicans who remained with the Church of England settled in Virginia and the Southern Colonies. They came to be known as the Episcopalians, as we saw in the last chapter. But the Episcopalians were handicapped during the Revolutionary War because they were under the English Government. Therefore, they organized as the **Protestant Episcopal Church of America** with their own local Bishops. Then during the early part of the nineteenth century, they divided themselves into three Bodies: **High Church, Broad Church** and **Low Church.**

The High Church resembles the Roman Catholic Church in worship and practice but does not accept the Pope. They have Tradition, along with Holy Scripture, as sources of Divine Knowledge. They have Seven Sacraments, teach that only Churches having Apostolic Succession are valid and have authority. **[It is the High Church that attempted to negotiate a union with the Eastern Orthodox Church in the early part of the twentieth century. However the attempts failed because they were not willing to sever relations with the Broad and Low Churches, which do not accept Holy Tradition, all Seven Sacraments and Apostolic Succession.]**

The Broad Church is more Protestant in character, accepts only Scripture, the Sacraments of Baptism and Eucharist, and has ritual and worship.

The Low Church is simply a Fundamentalist Church (one that accepts the teachings of the Bible in a literal sense), accepts Scripture, the Sacraments of Baptism and Eucharist, and has relatively little ritual and worship.

Orthodox Christians who migrated to America in the early part of the twentieth century and settled in the outlying cities and towns were misled by Protestant Episcopal Churches to believe that there were no basic differences between the two Churches. They were encouraged to attend those churches and to receive Holy Communion there. **[An Orthodox Christian cannot receive Holy Communion in a Non-Orthodox Church.]**

CONCLUSION

Thus far we have studied the Protestant Reformation and what Churches immediately emerged. In the next chapter we will discuss the American Protestant Churches as well as the American Non-Christian Churches.

CHAPTER TWENTY-FOUR

THE PROTESTANT REFORMATION IN AMERICA

Our Nation has been called Protestant America because of the religious impact the Protestant Churches made not only before and during the Revolutionary War, but right up to the turn of the twentieth century. Presbyterianism and Congregationalism imposed puritan thoughts on the New England Colonies, which influenced the Constitution of the United States and American culture and tradition. The Church of England entrenched itself in the Southern Colonies and introduced a country-gentleman culture on the pre-Civil South that still exists today. The Roman Catholic Church moved into Louisiana, New Mexico and the entire California coastline with churches, monasteries and missions. The Lutheran Church dominated the midwest as Germans and Scandinavians migrated to America. To these religious bodies already discussed must be added the Baptists who shaped the deep south; the Methodists and their circuit riders who rode across the Alleghenies with the pioneers; the Mormons of the Idaho-Utah territories; and the Non-Christian denominations, which although dramatically differ from Protestants, nonetheless emerged from the Protestant Reformation. We need to take a brief look at the most important ones.

BAPTIST CHURCH

The Baptists began as a Church in 1606 with John Smyth as their leader. They emerged from the Church of England. They stemmed from a group from Zwingli's time that rejected infant baptism; they were called "*Anabaptists*" (To be baptized again). The Baptists, as they came to be called, disavowed infant baptism and were re-baptized as adults, declaring that one should be baptized only after he is capable of believing.

The Early Christian Church believed in and practiced infant baptism because through it one's birthrights and citizenship in the Kingdom of God were restored. In other words, one began immediately practicing and living as a citizen in God's kingdom on earth at baptism, much in the same sense we begin being American citizens from birth or naturalization. This ancient practice has been kept by the Orthodox Church, the Roman Catholic Church and most of the Protestant Churches.

Roger Williams organized the First Baptist Church in America at Providence, Rhode Island in 1631. Since then the Baptists have divided and subdivided into many different groups, together constituting one third of all Protestants in America. Even though they are separated because of administrative policies and political differences, their doctrinal beliefs are basically the same. They lean heavily on Calvinist Predestination, profess to base all their doctrines and practices exclusively upon the Bible, declare an obedience and loyalty to Jesus Christ, and insist upon the freedom of the individual to approach God for himself. Baptists teach the Lutheran doctrine of Justification by Faith Alone, baptize adults by immersion, hold the Eucharist to be merely a symbolic practice and give absolute autonomy to each local church.

The Baptists have no hierarchy nor priesthood because they believe in the universality of the priesthood; that is to say, each individual is a priest since each one must approach God by himself or herself. Their ministers' duties and responsibilities are limited to preaching sermons, performing certain religious services, counseling and hospital visitation. Baptists are known for their hospitals, Homes for the Aged, Schools and Missions. There is a great controversy among Baptists today separating them into two groups. The vast majority hold to the basic doctrine of scripture and believe in the literal interpretation of scripture, and therefore, the inerrancy of scripture. Another group has emerged, primarily from some of the Baptist Seminary faculties, that believes there might be some places where scripture can be chronologically inaccurate. Some events and incidents need not necessarily be taken literally. Nevertheless, the entire Bible is inspired by the Holy Spirit and therefore is the record of God's truth. **[The latter is the teaching of the Orthodox Church also.]**

THE METHODIST CHURCH

The Methodist Church sprang from the Church of England, however much later than the Baptist Church. The word *"Methodist"* was originally a sarcastic barb in 1729 aimed by fellow students of Oxford University in England at the manner in which two brothers, John and Charles Wesley, and their friends pursued a strict way of living from dawn to bedtime. Their every action of study, prayer, Bible-reading and meditation was methodically planned to make them more godly. They were called Bible-bigots and Methodists --the last name stuck.

By 1740 John and Charles Wesley organized the first Methodist Church in England, and by 1766 it spread to New York. The Methodists had a difficult time at first because John Wesley upheld King George III's stand against the American Colonists. It was Francis Asbury, a Methodist missionary and American nationalist, who kept the Methodist Church from annihilation during the American Revolutionary War. The Methodists presented George Washington with a written pledge of allegiance at his inauguration, thus becoming the first Church to promise to support the new Nation. After the War of Independence the American Methodist Church became independent and was officially organized in 1784.

The Methodist Church is divided into twenty-three Methodist bodies in the United States today. Like the Baptists, they differ primarily in administrative policies rather than religious teachings. Their basic beliefs are: The Holy Trinity, the natural sinfulness of man, the need of a personal conversion based on genuine repentance of sins, Justification by Faith Alone, Baptism and Eucharist (although the latter is a symbolic commemoration and grape juice is used instead of wine), and a fundamentalist approach to the Holy Bible (a literal meaning to everything in the Bible). The Methodists do not believe in Calvinist Predestination. To the contrary, they insist upon the freedom of man's will. Methodists also believe in the universality of the priesthood; however they do have Bishops and regard them as supervisors of districts.

BLACK CHRISTIAN CHURCHES

Although some Protestant Churches in America did some missionary work, the Baptists and Methodists were the only Churches that concerned themselves with Christianizing the Negroes after the Civil War. Today 65% of all Black Christians are Baptists, 22% are Methodists and the rest are from the other denominations, including the Roman Catholic Church. The Black Christians found it easy to identify their plight with the Bible stories of the Old Testament. The refrains of the famous Negro spirituals reminded them of the oppressed people who had once conquered the Promised Land. How Daniel had been saved from the lions. How the Three Holy Children survived the fiery furnace. How David had slain Goliath. The Black Churches also supplied the desegregationalist movement with some of the most articulate leaders. One of the most famous, of course, was the late Baptist Minister, Dr. Martin Luther King, assassinated in 1968.

SEVENTH DAY ADVENTISTS

Adventist Churches believe that the Second Coming of Jesus Christ is the sole hope of the world. They hold that the world is evil and will be destroyed by divine intervention, and that the wicked are to perish while the righteous are to be saved. Basing themselves on Revelation 20:4-6, they believe that Jesus Christ will reign one thousand years with the saved ones.

Adventism began in Europe in the early part of the

nineteenth century. In America Adventism began as an interchurch movement with William Miller of Low Hampton, New York, as its leader. It included Methodists, Baptists, Presbyterians and Congregationalists. They calculated that the Day of Judgment would be October 22, 1844. When the day came and passed, those who remained formed the Seventh Day Adventist Church.

Seventh Day Adventists believe in the Holy Trinity, observe the Sabbath on Saturday (hence their title), hold the Bible as the only source of Divine Knowledge, Baptism by immersion and only for adults, little if any Eucharist, abstain from alcoholic beverages and tobacco, believe in the resurrection in the last day and immortality for the righteous, and utter destruction for the wicked. They stand for religious liberty and for complete separation of Church and State. Finally, they believe that Jesus Christ will come again in bodily form to live with the righteous for one thousand years.

CHURCH OF JESUS CHRIST OF LATTER DAY SAINTS: THE MORMONS

To the Main-Line Protestant Reformation Churches must be added those Churches which emerged from the Christian Churches but separated from them in basic Christian doctrine. One of these is the Church of Jesus Christ of Latter Day Saints: The Mormon Church.

Mormonism began as a laymen's movement with Joseph Smith as its organizer in 1830, at Fayette, New York. Smith claimed to have experienced a series of heavenly visitations in which he was informed that all existing Churches were in error; that the true Gospel was yet to be restored; that it would be revealed to him; and that he was to re-establish the true Church on earth which was to be called the **Church of Jesus Christ of Latter Day Saints.** He claimed he was led by an angel of the Lord to discover certain golden plates or tablets buried in a hill called Cumorah, near Manchester, New York. These tablets were left by an ancient prophet named Moroni and contained the sacred records of ancient inhabitants of America.

According to the Mormon Church, America was originally settled by the Jaredites, one of the groups dispersed during the confusion of tongues at the Tower of Babel. They claimed the American Indians were direct descendents of the Hebrews who came from Jerusalem in 600 B.C. Mormons also believe Jesus Christ visited this country after His Resurrection.

Once Joseph Smith found the plates he translated the hieroglyphic writings into the **Book of Mormon.** It is from the title of this Book that the word **"Mormon"** came into use. The golden plates were then returned to the angel of the Lord. Joseph Smith and his group reestablished the true Church. Smith was persecuted and put to death some time later. After his death a Quorum of Twelve was elected with Brigham Young as President. The Mormons settled in the Great Salt Lake Valley of Utah territory.

Mormons claim to believe in the Holy Trinity but they differ dramatically from Christian Trinitarian doctrine. They believe God the Father had twelve sons, two of which were Jesus and Satan. Jesus and Satan did battle and Jesus won. Those who followed Jesus became good and those who followed Satan became bad. They believe in baptism by immersion, the Eucharist each Sunday, tithing, visions, revelations and divine healing. Mormons also believe we all existed in a spirit world and were born into this world. Marriage is important because each couple will become god-husband and god-wife, will inhabit a planet in the next world, and eternally populate it with offspring.

CHRISTIAN SCIENCE

The Church of Christ Scientist was founded in 1879, in Boston, Massachusetts, by Mary Baker Eddy. Mrs. Eddy wrote ***Science and Health with Key to the Scriptures,*** which her followers consider equal in authority to the Holy Bible. She taught that God, being Spirit (mind), would not create anything unlike Himself. Therefore, man must be wholly spiritual (mental), without really having a material body that is subject to disease and death.

Jesus of Nazareth, understanding man's true nature, could heal people. His Resurrection proved that even death is unreal. Christian Scientists believe that people today, by using Christ's **"science,"** can free themselves of the *"illusion"* of sickness without needing medical aid. Sunday services consist of hymns, prayers and readings from *Science and Health* and from the Bible. Wednesday evenings people testify to the healings and other benefits which they believe they have experienced. At all times licensed *"practitioners"* pray for those suffering from the *"beliefs"* of sickness, though in reality they do not exist. Christian Science sees no distinction in essence between God and nature, Creator and creation, God and man, Christ's Human Nature and His Divine Nature. The basic biblical doctrine of man's Fall and his salvation in Christ are denied. Christian Science believes man is a spark of the Divine Fire of God striving mentally to realize his union with God. **Christian Science in no way can be considered a Christian Church.**

RELIGIOUS SOCIETY OF FRIENDS: QUAKERS

The Religious Society of Friends began with George Fox in England in 1654. Fox said, *"When all of my hopes in Churches and churchmen were gone, then I heard a voice which said, 'There is one, even Christ Jesus, that can speak to the condition'."* From this revelation he came to the conclusion that every person can be guided to the presence of God through an inner light, without worship or liturgical forms. He gathered others as followers and they called themselves the **Religious Society of Friends.** Once when Fox was arrested, he adjured the Magistrate to *"quake with fear of the Lord."* The Magistrate called him a *Quaker* and since that time the name **"Quaker"** has remained.

Quakers arrived in the New England Colonies in 1656.The first Society of Friends in America was organized in 1672 when George Fox came. Quakers have ministers and elders to govern their individual churches. Their worship consists of meditations and prayer. There are no sacraments, no pulpits, no altars nor church appointments. They have spontaneous prayer, scripture, testimony, preaching and singing as the spirit moves them. There are several Quaker Groups in America. **Quakers are not Christians because they do not believe in the Holy Trinity.**

JEHOVAH'S WITNESSES

Jehovah is the Hebrew word for God in the Old Testament. A group of Bible students wanting to witness for God were organized by Charles Taze Russell in Pittsburgh, Pennsylvania in 1872. Russell was not an ordained minister but became President of the group. Russell was succeeded by Judge Rutherford in 1916, who moved the headquarters to Brooklyn, New York. Rutherford gave his group the name of **Jehovah's Witnesses.**

Jehovah's Witnesses believe that God ruled at the beginning of the world but Satan rebelled and became ruler of the world. Mankind turned from God's happiness, peace and blessedness, and followed Satan. Then came Jesus Christ to end Satan's rule. Jesus' rule began in 1914, according to Jehovah's Witnesses. There will be a great battle at Armageddon where Satan will be defeated by Christ. Christ will emerge King and the righteous of the earth will reign with Him for one thousand years. They have predicted several dates but so far none have materialized. **While Jehovah's Witnesses claim some belief in Jesus Christ, they cannot be regarded as Christians.**

CONCLUSION

Protestant Churches came into being because of historical, political and doctrinal differences which appeared in Western Christendom. Had the Church of Rome retained the Conciliar tradition, had the reformers had the opportunity to confer with Eastern theologians, had the reformers remained within the framework of the teachings and practices of the Early Christian Church, perhaps they would not have evolved as they did. But the fact remains that there are some two hundred and fifty Protestant Denominations in America today. Once the break with the Traditional Church was made, each reformer considered it his privilege and prerogative to shape and fashion his new Church along the teachings and traditions he interpreted. **The Orthodox history student has the responsibility to not only scrutinize each Christian Church from an historical, doctrinal, scriptural and traditional viewpoint, but to present the Orthodox Church in Her proper perspective as well. It is simply not enough to be a Fundamentalist; to pick and choose at random which sacraments will be followed and which will be rejected; to regard the bread and wine of the Eucharist as symbolic and commemorative in one instance and the Body and Blood of Jesus Christ for the believer in another. Were Christian doctrine and commitment that simple, the Early Christians would not have held on to their tenets quite so tenaciously.**

The objective student of history must keep several points in mind:

–The traditions, practices and rituals that Protestants rejected were done so in direct opposition to the abuses noted in Western Christendom and not with Eastern Christendom.

–The fact that Protestants saw the Sacraments of Confession, Confirmation, Unction, Marriage and Priesthood misinterpreted and misconstrued in the West does not mean they should be rejected by the East.

–The fact that good works, penances and symbolic acts were misguided and used as means of soliciting funds for the Papal treasury does not reduce their intent and purpose for the Christian.

-The fact that Rome deviated from the Conciliar action of the Hierarchy and transformed it into a monolithic, central authority free from error does not mean that the Hierarchal structure of the Church should be totally rejected.

The following are some of the objections Protestants usually raise against Orthodox Christianity:

THE CHURCH

Some Protestants proclaim that "The Bible is God-given while the Church is man-made." St. Paul writes **" I hope to come to you soon, but I am writing these instructions to you so that, if I am delayed, you may know how one ought to behave in the househod of God, which is the church of the living God, the pillar and bulwark of the truth."** I Timothy 3:14-15. (See also Matthew 16:18, Acts 8:3, I Corinthians 4:17, Ephesians 1:22 and Colossians 1:18.)

HOLY TRADITION

Protestants accuse Orthodox Christians of giving equal authority to Tradition that is given to Scripture. St. Paul writes in II Thessalonians 2:15: ***"So then, brethren, stand firm and hold to the traditions which you were taught by us, either by word of mouth or letter."*** (See also Mark 7:6-16, Colossians 2:8 and II Thessalonians 3:6) **Jesus taught by word of mouth. The Apostles taught by word of mouth.** Saint Paul's Letters were a response to inquiries, problems and advice. The Gospels were collections of Jesus' parables, miracles and teachings which were gathered together. Copies of both the Letters and Gospels were circulated among the Christian Churches during the second half of the first century. Eventually the Successors of the Apostles [Bishops] gave authority and canonicity to what came to be known as the **Holy Bible.** In other words, it was **Holy Tradition, Unwrittten Scripture**, that not only preceded the Bible but gave authority to the Bible.

VIRGIN MARY THEOTOKOS

Protestants accuse Orthodox Christians of worshipping Mary. Orthodox Christians do not worship her; they venerate her and hold her in high esteem. Again, Scripture tells us in Luke 1:26-56 that She is the ***"favored one,"*** that She is the Mother of God because ***"the Child to be born [of Her] will be called holy, the Son of God,"*** and ***"Behold, henceforth all generations will call me blessed."***

The Holy Virgin Mary Theotokos stands as the greatest example of mankind's free response to God's offer of salvation. She stands as an example of God's will and mankind's acceptance --that unique cooperation between man and God. God did not force His will on Mary but waited for her faith response. She declared: ***"I am the Lord's Handmaiden: May it happen to me as you have said."***(Luke 1:38). Mary could have refused. She was not merely passive but an active participant in both the Mystery of God's will and the redemptive process of mankind's salvation. This is why she is venerated with love and great esteem.

THE SAINTS

Protestants also accuse Orthodox Christians of worshipping Saints and using them rather than praying directly to Christ. Orthodox Christians venerate Saints and look upon them as the **Church Triumphant** that comprises that part of God's Kingdom. Chapter 12 of Hebrews relates the whole cloud of saints, martyrs and witnesses both in the Old Testament times as well as Apostolic times. 12:22 reminds us of ***"the ecclesia [Church] of the first-born who are enrolled in heaven, and to a judge who is God of all, and to the spirits of righteous men made perfect."*** Scripture also tells us that both Enoch (Genesis 5:24 and Hebrews 11:5-6) and Elijah (II Kings 2:11) ascended into Heaven alive and in body form. We look to the angels, forefathers, prophets, apostles, martyrs and saints as role models and call upon them to intercede in our behalf.

ICONS

Protestants accuse Orthodox Christians of idolatry when it comes to the veneration of icons and the use of ecclesiastical vessels and articles in private and corporate liturgical experiential worship. In Orthodox theology icons are a **picture language theology.** They relate to us the record of God's truths through scenes and symbols just as the printed word does on the pages of the Bible. As far as ecclesiastical articles and symbols, we read in Exodus 25:19 how the Ark of the Covenant was adorned with cherub angels. Even Martin Luther, the Father of the Protestant Reformation, called on his flock to use the sign of the cross. In his Small catechism VII, 1, he instructs: *"In the morning, when you rise, make the sign of the cross and say, 'In the Name of God the Father, the Son, and the Holy Spirit. Amen'."*

Most Protestants think the Eastern Christian Church ceased to exist as a Church after 1054 A.D. They will recognize and admit that the East could produce theologians of stature (i.e., St. Basil the Great, St. Gregory the Theologian, St. Gregory of Nyssa, St. John Chrysostom, etc.) during the Golden Age but cannot seem to conceive that the East continued to be a strong Christian Church since then as well. The Orthodox Church continued to produce dynamic theologians, clouds of martyrs and saints, as well as spirit-filled Christians right up to our present time. Modern Orthodox Christians have a moral responsibility to become steeped in the history of the Church and bear witness to the Orthodox Faith.

ECUMENICAL DIALOGUE

Having said all this, the reader should also be aware that the mid-to-latter twentieth century has ushered in ecumenical and theological dialogue groups on international, national and local levels. Soberminded theologians have begun to discuss theological differences as well as similarities. More details are found in the last chapter.

CHAPTER TWENTY-FIVE

THE ROMAN CATHOLIC CHURCH

THE COUNTER-REFORMATION UNTIL TODAY

The Protestant Reformation had a slow start; but once it began, it swept across Central and Western Europe. By 1572 it reached its peak and began to suffer a recession. The Roman Catholic Church began checking and restraining the gains of Protestantism and slowly regained lost territories. This period in Church History is called the *Counter-Reformation.* The early reformers set their sights on reforming the hierarchy, the clergy and the laity of the Church. In some measure they accomplished their goals because Rome embarked on a three-fold reform program.

> 1) Discipline and reform became a must for all clergy and laity.
>
> 2) Doctrines and teachings were systematized, defined and published in the form of catechisms and distributed to the laity, while the clergy were required to obtain a college education.
>
> 3) Church administration and government underwent a complete reorganization while the See of Rome solidified her claims to Papal Supremacy.

These programs were introduced by the Council of Trent and enforced through the efforts of a newly-organized group of priests called *Jesuits*.

COUNCIL OF TRENT (1545-1563)

The Council of Trent was not convened through the initiative of the Pope but rather at the beckoning of certain political rulers in Germany who were in sympathy with Rome and wished to put a stop to the Protestant Movement in their provinces. It was convened in December of 1545 by Pope Paul III in the German city of Trent near the German-Italian border. The Spanish and French Bishops were willing to concede that the Bishop of Rome had a primacy of honor but that each Bishop drew his authority through Apostolic Succession and not through the Bishop of Rome alone. The Protestants were invited; but they refused to come, insisting that scripture be the sole authority for doctrine, faith and practice. Unfortunately, when the voting took place, the majority of Bishops present were either Italian Bishops or Bishops who favored papal authority. The greatest single force that influenced the Council of Trent was the Jesuit Movement.

The Jesuits insisted upon complete obedience and loyalty to the Pope.

The Council of Trent was another of those rare moments in the history of the West when the ancient practice of Conciliar action could have been restored, but it was defeated by default. Although the Council was designed to restore order to the Church and satisfy the Protestant Reformers, the Counter Reformation was too late to stop the Protestant Reformation. Instead of the Council of Trent returning to the Conciliar movement and instead of papal authority being diminished, the Popes emerged stronger and more powerful. The following is a synopsis of the decisions of the Council of Trent:

1) Holy Scripture and Holy Tradition are the two sources of Divine Knowledge and they have equal authority. The Old Testament is comprised of forty-nine books (which include Tobit, Judith, Wisdom of Sirach, Wisdom of Solomon, First Esra, Baruch, Epistle of Jeremiah and the Three Books of Maccabees). **[These are in full agreement with Orthodox theology.]** Scripture would be translated into the vernacular tongues and taught; however, Latin would remain the liturgical language.

2) Justification by faith alone is not enough; it must be augmented with good works. Predestination was unequivocally denounced as contrary to the tradition of the Church. **[This is in full agreement with Orthodox theology; however, the next sentence is not.]** Purgatory and the Treasury of Merits were re-emphasized.

3) The Seven Sacraments are absolutely necessary for salvation. **[The Orthodox Church is in full agreement.]**

4) The Pope is Christ's Vicar on earth. All ranks of the clergy must profess obedience to the Sovereign Roman Pontiff. **[The Orthodox Church disagrees.]**

VATICAN COUNCIL I (1870)

During the next three hundred years the Roman Catholic Church continued to tighten its hierarchal structure under the central authority of the Pope. Various Societies such as the Congregation for the Propagation of the Faith, Paulist Fathers, Maryknoll Fathers, Redemptionist Fathers, Sisters of Mercy and many other church organizations were founded and sent their members to Christianize, educate and serve as domestic and foreign missionaries.

In the latter part of the nineteenth century Pope Pius IX introduced the idea of an Ecumenical Council at which both Orthodox and Protestant representatives might attend. Neither accepted the invitation because attendance implied acceptance of Papal authority. Pope Pius IX convened the Council anyway in 1869-1870 in the Vatican where the doctrine of **Papal Infallibility** was officially adopted. The Vatican Council decreed: *"When the Roman Pontiff speaks from his papal throne, by virtue of his Apostolic and Petrine authority [successor of Peter and Vicar of Christ], what he defines as doctrine regarding faith or morals to be held by the Universal Church is to be regarded as infallible."*

A group of Bishops from Germany, Austria, Bohemia and Switzerland refused to adopt the new doctrine claiming that only when the full Body of Bishops was in session were decisions infallible. They came to be known as **Old Catholics.** Today there are still some remnants of the Old Catholics in Europe and America (especially Polish).

ROMAN CATHOLICS IN AMERICA

The first Roman Catholics to come to America were the French explorers who came south from Canada and north through the Mississippi Valley, as well as Junipero Serra who came up the California coastline from Mexico. The first Roman Catholic Church was established in Baltimore, Maryland, in 1634. However, the overwhelming Presbyterian, Congregational and Anglican Colonists prohibited them by law to go beyond the territories of Maryland and Virginia. These restrictions were not removed until after the Declaration of Independence in 1776. In 1808 Baltimore became the first American Roman Catholic Archdiocese with a Archbishop.

The influx of European Roman Catholics to America was slow for the next thirty years. But then two and one half million poured in from Ireland (potato famine) and Germany (persecutions) between 1840 and 1850. The next great influx came with the Immigration Period of 1890 and on. Roman Catholics established monasteries and convents, built churches, parochial schools and hospitals, and publishing houses. While the Protestants fought every move and opposed each new advancement, nevertheless the Roman Catholic Church in America grew and expanded as we know her today.

VATICAN II (1961-1965)

In January of 1959, Pope John XXIII made an dramatic announcement to the Bishops of the Roman Catholic Church. He said the Vatican Council of 1870 would reconvene. Thus Vatican II was convened in 1961 and lasted until 1965, two years after Pope John XXIII died and was succeeded by Pope Paul VI. While the intent was to ease tensions and antagonisms between Roman Catholicism and Eastern Orthodox, Protestants, Oriental Religions, Jews and pagans, very little really changed in theology and doctrine. For those wishing to study in further detail there are volumes and volumes available. For our purpose we will confine ourselves to only the following three issues:

1) Primacy of Peter

The chief dividing issue between Orthodoxy and Roman Catholicism remains **Papal Supremacy and Papal Infallibility.** The misinterpretation of Jesus' words *"Thou art Peter and upon this rock I shall build my Church"* (Matthew 15:15), has remained for twelve centuries the one single factor shaping the development of doctrine and Church government in the Roman Church.

From the Orthodox standpoint, the Bishop of Rome was regarded **Primus inter pares** (first among equals) by reason of his Bishopric being located in the capital city of the Roman Empire. His distinction had no connection whatsoever with the Apostle Peter. Once the transfer of the imperial city from Rome to Byzantium took place, the Bishop of Constantinople was given the same primacy of honor. However, a special primacy of honor was accorded the Bishop of Rome for the sake of antiquity. But in both instances, it was a **Primacy of Honor**, not a **Primacy of Authority!**

In spite of the exposure by Western scholars that the Isidorian Decretals and the Constantinian Donation were forgeries, these did not deter Vatican II from ultimately decreeing, *"Christ determined that on Peter He would build His Church; to him he promised the keys of the Kingdom of Heaven."* Therefore, in spite of the new ecumenical courtesies, Roman Catholics still uphold the theory of the **Petrine Promise** and regard the Bishop of

Rome as having **Papal Primacy and Papal Infallibility.** They still remain entrenched in their theological position.

2) Conciliar Action

At first it seemed the Bishops were to be given more autonomy in their own provinces and were to share more in the government of the total Church. But ultimately it was decreed that the Pope alone had final authority since it was to St. Peter and his successors that Christ entrusted the Church.

For the Roman Catholic Church to become a conciliar Church, she would have to divest herself of the whole notion of a divine central authority embodied in the Pope of Rome. She would have to revert to the ancient practice of self-governing Churches. In other words, Cardinals, Archbishops and Bishops would look upon the Pope of Rome as deserving honor, prestige and respect, but would in no way depend upon the Vatican for authority and permission to govern their individual Archdiocesan and Diocesan districts. The Cardinals of the leading cities of the United States would look upon the Pope of Rome as having a **Primacy of Honor**, but would in no way be subservient to Rome.

3) Uniate Churches

The Uniate Churches or Eastern Rite Roman Catholic Churches have always been a stumbling block in Eastern Orthodox-Roman Catholic relations. According to the canons of the **One, Holy, Catholic and Apostolic Church** before the Great Schism of 1054, one Bishop alone could preside over a given district or province. As we have seen in history, there were many incidents when Rome replaced and/or appointed another Bishop, Archbishop and even Patriarch in the East. During the Crusades of the eleventh through thirteenth centuries this happened in Constantinople, Jerusalem, Antioch and throughout the

Balkan Countries and Mediterranean Islands. It occurred once again after the False Union of the Council of Florence/Ferrera, Italy (1438-1439), but was never accepted in the East. To the contrary, the clergy and laity in the Orthodox East roundly rejected the False Union.

This type of unilateral practice evolved in the Slavic Uniate Movement of the fifteenth and sixteenth centuries and spread to the Middle East. These Christians are called *Eastern or Greek Catholics*. They include Ukrainians, Carpatho-Russians, Syrians, Armenians and Copts. The Uniates retain the beliefs and the worship of the Eastern Orthodox Church but accept the Pope as the Head of the Church. (The terms *Eastern* and *Greek* refer to the Orthodox practices which they are permitted to retain; i.e., liturgy, vernacular (national) language in worship, married clergy, icons, vestments, etc.)

With Vatican II it was hoped that the Roman Catholic Church would ease the tensions between East and West by dissolving the Uniate Churches. Instead, the Council decreed the folowing: *"Some religious orders and associations of the Latin Rite are working in Eastern districts, or among Easterners; they are earnestly recommended to increase the effectiveness of their apostolic work by setting up, as far as possible, houses, or even provinces of the Eastern Rite."*

The Roman Catholic Church ignored a unique opportunity in history to express genuine Ecumenism towards the East by recognizing the Ecumenical Patriarchate of Constantinople. Here is an ancient Church which served as a stonghold against the assaults of Persians and Arabs over a period of one thousand years. For four hundred years of dark oppression under the Turks, they held high the torch of Christendom. And yet, no mention was even made about the Ecumenical Patriarchate of Constantinople in Vatican II's allusion to the Eastern Churches.

CONCLUSION

The reader should not be left with the impression that all Roman Catholic theologians agree with the doctrines and teachings of Vatican I and Vatican II. There are many Western theologians wrestling with the problems of Papal Primacy, Papal Infallibility, the Roman Catholic Eucharist, ecclesiology and moral theology. Also there are many Roman Catholic clergy and laity today who are interested in learning about the ancient Church and the perpetuation of her doctrinal and liturgical practices. This is all the more reason why we need enlightened, knowledgeable, dedicated and fortified Orthodox Christians in America today. This is why it is so important for you, the reader, to learn the teachings and liturgical practices of the Orthodox Christian Church. You have a very special role to play in the development, expansion and perpetuation of the Orthodox Christian Faith in America.

CONCLUDING CHAPTERS

The last six chapters have dealt with the Development of the Papacy, the Protestant Reformation, the Calvinist Movement, the Counter-Reformation, and Vatican I and II Councils —essentially, what occurred in Western Christendom (Roman Catholicism and Protestantism). The last six chapters will touch upon what occurred in Eastern Christendom during this same period of time. The emergence of Orthodox Christianity to the American Continent in particular will be discussed. The last chapter will bring into focus the role and participation of the Orthodox Church in the Ecumenical Movement.

CHAPTER TWENTY-SIX

GREEK ORTHODOX CHURCH: 1453-1821

Western historians generally date 1492 as the dividing point between the Middle Ages and the Modern Age in political history, and 1517 in Church History. The Eastern Orthodox Church historian would have to set 1453 as the dividing point. S.M. Sophocles, in his *History of Greece* states the following:

> *"The Fall of Constantinople on May 29, 1453, marked a new epoch in world history. The empire which had inherited the lofty traditions of the Graeco-Roman world and sheltered the magnificence of classical civilization, championed Christianity, and instilled justice into law, was shattered by the might of the Crescent. Byzantium, the barrier and the salient outpost of Europe against Asia, succumbed, and the Turks entrenched themselves in the bastions of Constantinople which became their capital and was named 'Istanbul.' With Mohammed II, a new era was established on the shores of the Mediterranean." (p.145)*

The Fall of Constantinople opened the door to conquest after conquest by the Turks. First in the East, Bulgaria, Albania, Moldavia, Walachia, Serbia, the Ukraine and the Caucasus fell, one after another. From the East they crossed the Danube and entered the Western world, conquering Hungarian and Austrian territories. The Ottoman Turks menaced the West and Russian territories for another two centuries before their empire went into decline. But what was for the West a menacing threat, for the Orthodox Greeks and other Balkan Orthodox was an intolerable yoke which lasted for four hundred years.

Most Western writers accuse the Greek Orthodox Church of having been dormant and stagnant since 1453. The mere fact that the Church survived the myriad sufferings, tyrannies and massacres during those four centuries should indicate that she was anything but dormant and stagnant. In spite of indignities, humiliations and injustices, the Church did not succumb. It was the Greek Orthodox Church that not only preserved Orthodoxy throughout Asia Minor (present day Turkey) and the Balkans, but also cultivated and perpetuated the spirit of nationalism which eventually liberated the Orthodox people from the shackles of bondage and slavery. This chapter will deal with some of the problems which the Greek Orthodox Church encountered while under the Turkish Yoke.

BYZANTINE GREEKS UNDER TURKISH YOKE

The Ottoman Yoke fell heaviest upon the Byzantine Greeks in Asia Minor, the mainland of Greece and the Islands. Greece, the Ionian and Aegean Islands were constantly in the crossfire battles between the Turks and the Spanish or the Italians (Venetians, Genoese). In addition to the regular harassment they had to tolerate while under the Turkish Yoke, they were also subjected to retaliations, being taken as hostages and forced to serve their captors. The Greeks in Asia Minor were closer to the heart of the Empire and consequently were constantly under the threat of danger from treachery and intrigue.

The Muhammedans did not allow the conquered people any liberty, but they did permit them to worship because the Koran made allowances for it. They grouped all the Orthodox Christians into one nation which they called **Rum Millet**, Greek Nation, regardless of whether they were Greeks, Arabs, Serbs, Bulgarians, Albanians or Ukrainians. The Patriarch of Constantinople became the officially recognized Ethnarch who was both Hierarch and Judge. The position of the Patriarch was both an exalted and a precarious one because each knew he held the office only so long as he retained the good will and favor of the Muslim rulers.

Another threat to the Patriarchate came about from the special practice of giving a sizeable monetary gift to the

Sultan when seeking his approval of the election and appointment of a Patriarch. This practice resulted in frequent changes, chronic intrigues and violent ends for a good many Patriarchs. During the four hundred years of Turkish domination only twenty-one of the one hundred and fifty-nine Patriarchs died a natural death. The others were either forced into exile and hardship or put to death. But even though the Church suffered greatly, it was the Patriarchate of Constantinople, as well as the Bishops and Priests throughout Asia Minor and the Balkans, who not only preserved Orthodoxy but cultivated and perpetuated the spirit of nationalism which eventually brought about the Greek War of Independence in 1821.

DECLINE OF THE OTTOMAN EMPIRE AND THE ROLE OF THE PHANARIOTES

By the latter part of the seventeenth century the Ottoman Empire began to decline in power and ceased to be a threat any longer. They divided the Empire into Provinces and Districts and appointed subordinates to rule them. They also recruited men from the conquered nations to share in the administrative responsibilities. For example, in Constantinople the Turks used Greeks as contractors, architects, shipbuilders, bankers, merchants and in key government positions. Out of this task force emerged a powerful group of Greeks called **Phanariotes.** The Phanariotes took their name from **Phanar**, the lighthouse quarter of the old city of Constantinople. The Phanar used to be a lighthouse on the south shore of the Golden Horn. After Muhammed II converted Saint Sophia into a mosque in 1453,the Patriarchate was located at different sites in the City. Finally, in 1601 the Patriarchate was relocated in the Phanar District, where it remains until this present day with the Church of St.George as the Patriarchal Church. The Phanariotes were a tremendous help to the Patriarchate of Constantinople. Although they did not plan nor carry out the Greek Revolution in 1821, nevertheless, they rendered invaluable service in its preparation and execution.

THE ORTHODOX CHURCH AND PROTESTANTISM

During the middle 1570's Patriarch Jeremiah II was approached by some German Lutheran theologians to comment on a Greek copy of the Augsburg Confession. This confession contained articles of faith stating that Holy Scripture alone is the sole source of Divine Knowledge, that only the Sacraments of Baptism and Eucharist were acceptable and that Justification by faith alone was sufficient. The document also had overtones of predestination and other Protestant arguments in it. Jeremiah sent an answer back to the Lutheran theologians, disagreeing with them and refuting each of the articles of the Augsburg Confession. He told them they did not have the authority to pick and choose only those teachings of the Fathers which they wanted nor to interpret Scripture as they wished. He concluded by inviting them to return to Orthodoxy --the Church of the Ecumenical Councils!

A NEW ERA OF NATONALISM

The latter part of the eighteenth century ushered in a new era of nationalism and the spirit of revolution. The quest for independence was everywhere. America declared her independence in 1776 and fought for it against England. The French Revolution began in 1789 and the Spanish in 1820. New States and New Nations such as Austria, Prussia, Italy, Sweden and Poland emerged. The Greeks, who had long perpetuated the spirit from one generation to another, waited with eager anticipation for the right opportunity.

The latter part of the eighteenth century also marked a change in the attitude of the Turks in and around Constantinople. While Napoleon was planning a United Europe, the

Turks began implementing a more humane and liberal policy towards their subjects. The Greek Orthodox Church was permitted once again to exercise those prerogatives which were accorded by Muhammed II. More schools were allowed to open in Constantinople and the surrounding areas. The Turkish government allowed the well-trained Greeks of Constantinople to conduct the affairs of politics and diplomacy, both at home and abroad. Alexander Mavrocordatos, a member of a prominent Greek family, became Grand Vizier, Prime Minister of the Sultan's Council. Greeks in and around Constantinople became financially prosperous. This was also the century for secret societies in Western and Eastern Europe. Out of this wealthy and influential group of Constantinopolitan Greeks emerged a society called **Philiki Hetairia**, Society of Friends. (The Greek Philiki Hetairia was in no way connected nor affiliated with the Quakers' Society of Friends.)

The **Philiki Hetairia** began as an underground movement during the latter part of the eighteenth century. The Society grew in members and spread to include Greeks and Philhellenes in Russia, France, Austria, Italy and England. It was the Society of Friends which secretly prepared for the revolution. They set up an intricate network of messengers who disseminated literature and poetry, stirred up patriotic sentiment and marshaled troops, equipment and funds. By 1814 the Society of Friends emerged as a formidable political and militant organization.

MARCH 25, 1821

Once the wheels of the revolution were in motion, there was no turning back. Greece felt that the time was ripe. They could wait no longer. Poets and writers like Adamantios Koraes encouraged and incited the people to declare in spirit and action those immortal words: *"better one hour of freedom than forty years of slavery and bondage."* Thus they selected March 25th, the Feast Day of the

Annunciation, as the day to herald the revolution. The Archangel Gabriel came to the Virgin Mary and announced that She was to give birth to the Christ Child, Who was to liberate humanity from the bondage of sin. What better day was there for the Greeks to announce to the Turks and to the world that they were ready to cast off the shackles of their intolerable yoke! Thus the insurrection began in interest in the Peloponnesus, when on March 25, 1821, Germanos, the Metropolitan Bishop of the Old See of Patras, Greece, blessed some of the leaders and they set off for their quest to liberate their homeland. In a few months all of Greece was in full revolt.

THE APPEAL OF THE MESSINIAN SENATE

At first Greece did not have a central government to coordinate the fighting or to unify efforts and appeals. As time went on and Greek Provinces were liberated, they emerged as independent under local governments. The first such government body was the Messinian Senate, which wrote an appeal to the United States of America for recognition as a Modern State. The Messinian appeal was well received by the new American Government and the American people. Committees of American Philhellenes were formed, supportive resolutions were passed in Congress and fund-raising drives were initiated throughout the States. Many Americans went and fought in the Greek Revolution; one about whom we will read later was Dr. Samuel Gridley Howe.

PATRIARCH GREGORY V MARTYRED

When the news of the Greek revolt reached Constantinople, the Turks became outraged. They put to death countless Bishops, Priests, Nuns and Greek citizens of the highest rank. Properties were confiscated, and wives and daughters were sold in slavery. On the Island of Chios alone, 40,000 Greeks were massacred. They seized

Patriarch Gregory V as he celebrated the Paschal Liturgy, and they hanged him at the front gate of Patriarchate. Patriarch Gregory's Martyrdom inspired Greek freedom fighters to greater bravery.

GREECE BECOMES A NATION

The Greeks fought desperately for three years while Russia, England, France, Austria and Prussia watched apathetically and dispassionately. In February of 1824, England finally became sympathetic and issued her first loan to Greece. Tsar Alexander was succeeded by Tsar Nicholas I in 1826. On July 6, 1827, England, France, and Russia set up a treaty which stipulated that they should mediate between the contending Greeks and Turks. The Sultan refused, saying, *"My positive, absolute, definitive, unchangeable, eternal answer is, that the Sublime Sultan does not accept any proposition regarding the Greeks, and will persist in its own will regarding them even to the last day of judgment."*

England, France and Russia sent battleships to aid the Greeks in their valiant struggle for freedom. The result of the intervention of the three great powers was the decisive Battle of Navarino (October 20, 1827). The battle was a total defeat for the Turks. In September of 1829, after three and one-half centuries of oppression, Turkey finally acknowledged the Independence of Greece and recognized her as a Nation with full diplomatic status. At this time only the southern part of Greece was liberated. It took another seventy-five years for the rest of Greece, the Balkans (Albania, Rumania, Yugoslavia and Bulgaria), the Mediterranean Islands and the Middle East (Lebanon, Syria, Palestine, etc.) to be liberated. These areas were freed primarily after the First World War with the collapse of the Austro-Hungarian Empire, the Russian Empire and the Ottoman Empire. This also gave peoples from these geographic areas the freedom to immigrate to America as well.

CONCLUSION

Regardless of how objective one tries to be in studying the Greek Revolution of 1821, he must be impressed with the intrepid, dauntless and heroic determination of the Greeks against insurmountable odds. Not only are we who are of Greek, Balkan, Asia Minor and Middle Eastern extraction indebted to our ancestors and forefathers, but Europe and ultimately America as well. The Byzantine Empire helped hold back the Muslims up through the middle of the fifteenth century. In the fifteenth century millions of scholars fled from Byzantium to the West. Educators and historians contend that these scholars of the East contributed to the seed of the Renaissance and the development of Western Civilization from 1500 and forward. That civilization was first brought to America in the 1600's and 1700's and then later in the nineteenth and twentieth centuries. One can note the influence in architecture, culture and the arts throughout America. However, there is something here that is even more consequential and significant: Had it not been for the tenacity and heroism of men and women of the Greek Revolution, Greece, the Balkans, Asia Minor and the Middle East would not have been freed. Furthermore, our parents, grandparents and ancestors could not have come to America; and we would not have been born here. And had they not immigrated to America they would not have brought the Eastern Orthodox Christian Faith from their homelands. We all should be spiritually proud of this religious and cultural heritage ---it is a glorious one!

CHAPTER TWENTY-SEVEN

SLAVIC ORTHODOX CHURCHES: 1453-1917

Constantinople fell to Muhammed II on Tuesday, May 29, 1453. During the next two centuries Islam pressed hard into the Balkans, Southern and Central Europe. The Aegean Islands were soon conquered, and by 1538 the entire coast of the Black Sea fell. Shortly before that, the Turkish forces under the leadership of Suleiman the Magnificent had come within fifty miles of Vienna, Austria. But by the eighteenth century the Ottoman Empire began its decline and steady retreat from the West. The Orthodox Churches in Asia Minor, the Balkan States and the Middle East were not liberated until the latter nineteenth and early twentieth centuries. However, during this dark period for Eastern Orthodoxy, there was one nation in Eastern Christendom which remained free; and that was Russia.

THE RUSSIAN ORTHODOX CHURCH 1480-1917

The Mongolian Yoke, dating back to Genghis Khan's conquest of all Russia in 1240, came to an end in 1480 when Ivan III, the Great (1462-1505) of Moscow, refused to pay tribute taxes. Moscow replaced Kiev as the capital during the Tatar occupation. The Bishop's See was also transferred from Kiev to Moscow. In spite of their subjugation the Russians not only kept alive the religious heritage they received from the Byzantines, but they developed their own unique piety and spirituality as well. Nicolas Zernov in his book *Eastern Christendom* eloquently describes it in this manner:

"The Russia of Kiev was a young and enthusiastic disciple of Byzantium; the Russia of Moscow was a Christian outpost of the Asiatic world. It was behind Europe in science, in military and technical skill, but

there was one domain where the Russians were masters, and that was the sphere of worship understood as covering all aspects of personal, social and national life. In that art of Christian conduct described by the Russians as 'bitove blagochestie' (the piety of daily life) the Muscovites were unrivalled. Orthodoxy, etymologigically understood as 'True Glory' (Provoslavie), permeated their whole culture. The Russians achieved a remarkable spiritual unity. Tsars and boyars, merchants and peasants, all were members of the same Orthodox community, speaking the same language, sharing the same ideal, observing the same pattern of behaviour and completely understanding each other.

"Their inspiration came from their belief in the Incarnation, confirmed by the drama of the Eucharist, performed on each feast day by the entire nation. The Parish Church was the Russian's university, their concert hall, their art gallery, and above all the holy place, which reminded them that this world, in spite of its imperfections, was the temple of the Holy Spirit, and that man's vocation was to work for its transfiguration. The bright cupulas of the Russian Church adorned with golden crosses, the innumerable ikons depicting the triumphant Saints, the joy of Easter celebrations, all these typical manifestations of Russian Christianity eloquently declared the determination of the Russian people to sanctify their national life and uplift it to holiness and brotherly love." (p.141)

In 1448 a Council of Russian Bishops elected the Metropolitan of Moscow from one of their Bishops. Up to that time the Bishop of Moscow was a Greek Bishop appointed by the Patriarch of Constantinople. From that point on Moscow began operating as an Independent Church. In 1589 Jeremiah II, Patriarch of Constantinople, visited Moscow and declared it a Patriarchate. He consecrated Metropolitan Job the Patriarch of Moscow and All Russia.

PETER THE GREAT (1682-1725)

Peter the Great was responsible for modernizing Russia and expanding her territories. But he was also responsible for abolishing the Patriarchate of Moscow in 1721 when he replaced it with a Synod of Bishops to be nominated and dismissed by the Tsar. The Synod was submissive to the Tsar and always met in the presence of a secular official appointed by the Tsar.

RUSSIAN SPIRITUALITY

The eighteenth and nineteenth centuries heralded a great spiritual revival period in the Russian Church. This revival in iconography, architecture and literature came to be known as Russian Spirituality. It was during this time that St. Serapheim of Sarov (1759-1833), a Russian mystic, appeared. Another holy man was Father John Sergiev of Kronstadt (1829-1908), whose book *"My Life in Christ"* has remained a religious classic. And it was also a period of time when Orthodox missionaries like Bishop Innocent (John Veniaminov 1797-1879) went to the Aleutian Islands and Alaska and brought the message of Jesus Christ as perpetuated in the Orthodox Church through the Ages. This, too, will be discussed in a later chapter. For now let us quickly review the other National Orthodox Churches during the four centuries which followed the Fall of the Byzantine Empire.

THE SERBIAN CHURCH

The Serbian Church suffered the same consequences as did the other Balkan States under the conquering Turks. Although the Serbian Church had been given autonomy and independence in 1221 by the Byzantine Emperor Theodore Lascaris, nevertheless, they found it necessary to align themselves with the Ecumenical Patriarchate during the Turkish subjugation. Eventually, in 1897 the Serbian

Church was given official autocephalous status (self governing). However, the Serbian Church was not without its internal conflicts and divisions. With the territorial growth of the Austro-Hungarian Empire, parts of northern Serbia were annexed; and Roman Catholicism was imposed upon them. As a result, the Orthodox Christians were constantly harassed and oppressed. After the First World War and the dissolution of the Austro-Hungarian Empire, Serbia regained most of her territory along with parts of Albania, northern Greece and Austria. In 1922 the Orthodox Church of Serbia was raised to the rank of Patriarchate with Belgrade as its Seat. With the turn of the twentieth century many Serbian Orthodox immigrated to America and eventually founded Parishes, built churches and organized a Diocese under the sanction and jurisdiction of the Patriarchate of Belgrade.

THE ROMANIAN CHURCH

The Romanian Orthodox Church had its origen in the great works of the ninth-century missionary brothers, Sts. Cyril and Methodius. Romanians, too, suffered under the Turkish Yoke. When Russia defeated Turkey in a war in 1828-1829, the Provinces of Wallachia and Moldavia were liberated. These two Provinces were mainly inhabited by Romanians. In 1862 the two Provinces were recognized by the Great Powers (France, England, Austria and Russia) as the Nation of Romania.

The Romanian Orthodox Church had always been under the jurisdiction of the Patriarchate of Constantinople. It petitioned for independence, and in 1885 Romania was given autocephalous status. Later, in 1925, the Ecumenical Patriarchate of Constantinople elevated Romania to a Patriarchate with its Seat in Bucharest. Like the Serbs and the other Orthodox countries, Romania constructed beautiful churches, outstanding monasteries and founded many notable theological schools. Also like the other National Orthodox Churches, Romania, too, founded churches in America with the Immigration of Romanian Orthodox Christians.

THE BULGARIAN ORTHODOX CHURCH

While the Bulgarian Orthodox Church traces her origin and religious heritage back to the ninth century, she was one of the last Orthodox Churches to achieve independence and Patriarchal status. Geographically, Bulgaria was nearest Turkey and therefore was one of the last nations to be liberated from the Turkish Yoke. In 1875-1876, Russia came to the aid of the Bulgarians in an uprising against the Turks. Unfortunately, the Great Powers partitioned Bulgaria into three sections, returning the largest to the Sultan.

The Bulgarian Church had been given the status of self-governing church and for some time even a Patriarchate before the Fall of Constantinople in 1453. But it will be recalled that the Turks put all Orthodox Christians in conquered countries under the authority of the Ecumenical Patriarchate of Constantinople. When Bulgaria was reunited and recognized as a Nation, they demanded recognition as a Patriarchate from Constantinople. As a result of Constantinople's refusal, the two Churches remained in schism until 1945, when Bulgaria petitioned once again and was granted Patriarchal status with Sofia as the Seat.

Bulgaria has some of the most ancient churches and monasteries in which Byzantine art and iconography are still found in their original form. Ochrida, the ancient capital of Bulgaria, remains a storehouse of these priceless treasures and articles. Bulgarian Orthodox churches were founded in America with the immigration of Bulgarian people early in the twentieth century.

THE UKRAINIAN CHURCH

The Orthodox Churches of Western Poland, Lithuania and the Ukraine were canonically dependent on the Patriarchate of Constantinople. Their geographic location, however, constantly placed them under pressure and duress from the Kings of Poland to become Roman Catholics and fall under the See of Rome. In 1596 the Metropolitan Bishop Michael of Kiev, along with the majority of the Ukrainian Bishops, signed an act of union with Rome at Brest-Litovsk. This was the beginning of what came to be known as the **Uniate Churches** (unitas --the Latin word for unity). The Uniate Churches, also called Greek Catholics because they followed the Byzantine Rites, were permitted to keep their Orthodox churches, iconography, Byzantine Rite services, Slavonic language, customs, etc. Since it was the practice for their clergy to be allowed to marry before ordination, this, too, was retained. The only requirement imposed upon the clergy and laity was that they pledge their obedience and loyalty to the Pope of Rome.

However a significant group of Ukrainian Bishops, priests and laity remained Orthodox. In 1686, as a result of Russian victories over Poland, the Ukraine was annexed to Russia; and the Ukrainian Church was attached to the Patriarchate of Moscow with Constantinople's approval. As a result, a large part of the Uniates returned to Orthodoxy. As we shall see in a later chapter, thousands of Uniates also returned to Orthodoxy under the Patriarchate of Constantinople. In the United States today there are both Ukrainian Uniate Churches and Ukrainian Orthodox Churches.

ALBANIAN CHURCH

In 1912 Bulgaria, Serbia and Greece fought a war against Turkey and defeated her. Albania emerged as a Modern State. The Orthodox Christians of that territory formerly were part of the Patriarchate of Constantinople. In 1937 the Albanian Orthodox Church was given autocephalous status. After the Second World War Communism took over Albania and the Albanian Orthodox Church has continued to suffer ever since. Albanian Orthodox Christians immigrated to America at the turn of the century and founded churches in major cities.

CHAPTER TWENTY-EIGHT

THE EASTERN ORTHODOX CHURCH

ON THE AMERICAN CONTINENT

Thus far we have studied about the Early Christian Church and the political, historical and doctrinal issues that brought about the separation of the **One, Holy, Catholic and Apostolic Church.** The principal divisions are: **Eastern Orthodoxy, Roman Catholicism and Protestantism.** We have witnessed the appearance of Roman Catholic and Protestant Churches in America with the Pilgrims and the early settlers. But when did the Eastern Orthodox Christians reach the soil of the New World? Were there Orthodox Pilgrims and settlers? When did they apppear on the American scene? When did the Eastern Orthodox Church come to the American Continent?

EARLY RUSSIAN MISSIONARIES

The Eastern Orthodox Church in America received its foundation from the Russian Church when a Russian Orthodox Mission was sent to Alaska in the latter part of the eighteenth century. Peter the Great sent a Russian Naval Expedition to explore the Russian waters of the Arctic Ocean. The expedition, under the command of Vitus Bering, left Russia in 1725. One of the waterways discovered was the 36-mile stretch of water between Siberia and Alaska, called the Bering Strait, after the commander of the expedition. In 1741 Bering sailed again and discovered Alaska.

Fifty years later, a Russian Mission of eight monks of the Valaam Monastery arrived at Kodiak Island and built the first Orthodox Church there in 1794. During the first two years they baptized 12,000 natives and built several chapels. One of those monks was Father Herman, who died in 1837, after living an ascetic life on Spruce Island.

Father Herman was proclaimed the first American Saint on August 9, 1970, by the Russian Orthodox Church.

Although the bulk of Russian missionary endeavor was concentrated in the Alaska mainland and the Aleutian Islands (at that time belonging to Russia) nevertheless, missionaries moved in a southward direction to the California coastline. The first Orthodox Chapel to be built in California territory was at Fort Ross in 1812, just north of San Francisco. Unfortunately the chapel was destroyed by fire October 5, 1970. However, a replica has been constructed on the original site.

FATHER JOHN VENIAMINOFF: BISHOP INNOCENT

The single person most instrumental, the *"Cyril and Methodius"* to the Aleuts, the individual most responsible for the spread of Orthodox Christianity on the northwestern tip of the North American Continent was Father John Veniaminoff. He arrived at the Island of Unalaska, the second largest island of the Aleutian Archipelago, in 1824. During his first ten years he learned the language and customs of the Aleuts. He also wrote an Aleut grammar, translated the Divine Liturgy, Catechism and Gospel of Matthew with his Aleut grammar. He baptized practically all the inhabitants of the Island, whose ancestors for the most part have remained Orthodox until today. Father Veniaminoff settled in Sitka, Alaska, in 1834 and continued his missionary work there until 1839, when he returned to Russia for a brief stay. While in Russia he was ordained Bishop of Alaska, with the name Innocent. He returned to Sitka in 1841, where the Diocese was founded. In 1867, Alaska was sold to the United States by Russia for the sum of $7,200,000. Through the concerted efforts of Bishop Innocent provisions were stated that the United States recognize the property and the rights of the Russian Orthodox Church, and that the Church maintain the right to continue her missionary work.

Once Alaska and the Aleutian Islands became United States Territory, Orthodox missionary work spread to the California coastline. A Russian priest was sent to organize the *"Greek-Russian-Slavonian Orthodox Eastern Church of San Francisco."* At the beginning all the Orthodox in San Francisco worshipped together; but by the last decade of the nineteenth century, Greek immigrants began to flood the west coast, as they did the East and Central cities of the country. In 1904, the Greek Orthodox Church of Holy Trinity was founded. But this was not the first Greek Orthodox Church in the United States nor were the San Francisco Greeks the first to come to America.

GREEK AMERICANS BEFORE THE IMMIGRATION PERIOD

The first record of Greeks on American soil came in the middle of the eighteenth century. In 1767 the Colony of New Smyrna was founded on the eastern side of the Florida coastline by a Scotsman, Dr. Andrew Turnbull. The colony was named after his wife, Maria, the daughter of a Greek merchant in Smyrna, Turkey. In 1766, Turnbull was given 20,000 acres of uncultivated land by the English government. In the Spring of 1767, Turnbull went to Mani, Greece, where he paid the Provincial Governor 400 silver lyra for two hundred men. (It will be remembered that Greece was still under the Turkish Yoke and that it was not unusual for men to be bought and sold like merchandise.) He recruited an additional thirteen hundred men from Italy and Corsica. He returned to Florida the summer of 1768.

The recruits were given free passage on ship, room and board at the Smyrna Colony, and were contracted to labor without wages for three years. At the end of three years they were to have been given free title to fifty acres of land. But Turnbull did not honor the terms of his contract. In fact, the laborers suffered from heat, mosquitoes, exhaustion, bad food and from the oppression of their overseers, who treated them like the Negro Slaves of Georgia and the Carolinas. The Greek slaves stole away a few at a time to St. Augustine, a few miles to the north.

GREEKS IN ST. AUGUSTINE

St. Augustine is considered to be the oldest city in the United States. A 1793 census revealed that some one hundred Greek residents were registered at the time. Perhaps the most outstanding Greek name connected with the early St. Augustine settlement was John Giannopoulos. Giannopoulos is listed in the St. Augustine Registry of 1789 as having filed a license for marriage. The records clearly state that he was born in Mani, Greece,which would date him as one of the New Smyrna recruits. The house of John Giannopoulos in St. Augustine is considered to be the oldest standing school house in the United States. To this day the building is called, *"Giannopoulos School."* The Greek Orthodox Archdiocese of North and South America constructed the St. Photius Shrine Chapel at St. Augustine in memory of the Greek Pilgrims to the American Continent.

OTHER GREEKS BEFORE THE IMMIGRATION PERIOD

There are many Greeks who came to America long before the beginning of the Immigration Period at the turn of the twentieth century. During the nineteenth century, moreover, after the Greek War of Independence in 1821, many Greek lads were either sent to America by their parents to study and then return to their homeland, or were brought by American Missionaries and adopted by American families. Since most of the American Colleges at the time were religious institutions, hundreds of them became Protestant Ministers and/or Missionaries. Others became teachers, educators, scholars and officers in the Armed Forces. Although these young men were of Greek extraction, nonetheless, in most cases they did not reflect their Greek identity. Nor did they practice the religion of their forefathers, the Greek Orthodox Faith. Perhaps the major reason for their absorption into the mainstream of America, and their religious and ethnic oblivion, can be noted in the conspicuous absence of a Greek Orthodox Church and priest. The first to recognize these primary needs were the Greek merchants of the Import-Export Houses.

FIRST GREEK ORTHODOX CHURCH IN AMERICA

During the nineteenth century, Greek merchants were primarily in England, Russia, Egypt and India. In 1851, the House of Rallis opened a branch office in New York, New Orleans, and Savannah to import foreign goods and to export cotton. By the 1860's quite a few Greek cotton merchants were residing in New Orleans with their families. In 1866 with the initiative of Marinos Benakis, they organized a parish and built a chapel at 1222 North Dorgenois Street and named it in honor of the Holy Trinity. The New Orleans Church was the first Greek Orthodox Church founded in America. The small wooden structure served for eighty-four years and was replaced with a new church a short distance away in 1950.

Other churches were organized and buildings constructed in the 1890's, when the actual Immigration Period for the Greeks commenced. (Holy Trinity, New York, and Holy Trinity, Chicago, in 1892.) But as we shall see, with the emergence of the Greek immigrants and the appearance of the Greek Orthodox Church in America, the transition and adjustment was an extremely difficulty one. Many problems, dissensions and their repercussions affected the development and progress of the Church. These will be discussed in a later chapter.

ASSESSMENT OF ORTHODOXY IN AMERICA

The Russian Orthodox Missionaries were on the west coast when the English and Dutch Colonists were on the east coast. The Greeks in Florida were there before the American Revolution, as were the Greeks in New Orleans before the Louisiana Purchase. Greeks participated in every facet of American life during the nineteenth century. The fact that many of these Greeks assimilated into Roman Catholicism and Protestantism, or remained without any religious affiliation at all, bears out more explicitly the historical lesson we have to learn. Without an Orthodox Church, without an Orthodox priest, without the religious and cultural heritage which is ours, there is no hope for retaining, maintaining and perpetuatingthe rich Orthodox Christian heritage of the early Church. Nor the Patristic Church, nor the centuries-old

ONE, HOLY, CATHOLIC AND APOSTOLIC CHURCH!

We are not only the descendents of our ancestors and forebearers; we are their successors! Ours is a noble and responsible charge: To become dedicated Orthodox Christians and achieve our theosis and salvation! To pass on this legacy to our children and our children's children! And to make the Orthodox Christian Faith available for all non-Orthodox Americans who grope and search that they, too, may embrace it and find their religious fulfillment!

The Orthodox Church has a tremendous contribution to make on the American scene! We have said this over and over. However, if this contribution is to bear fruit it will require a great deal of enlightened, knowledgeable, inspired and spirit-filled Orthodox Christians!

CHAPTER TWENTY-NINE

EASTERN ORTHODOX CHURCHES: 1914-TODAY

The First World War caused the collapse of four Empires: They are the Russian, German, Austro-Hungarian and Ottoman. Their demise led to drastic changes in the life and destiny of all Eastern Orthodox Christians. What was left of the Ottoman Empire became the Modern State of Turkey. The harassment that continued both to the Christian residents and the Ecumenical Patriarchate will be discussed in another chapter. This chapter will discuss the Slavic, Balkan and Middle East Orthodox Christian Churches as they evolved after the First World War, and how they came to America.

RUSSIA

In 1917 the Russian Tsarist Government fell to the Communist Party. Vladimir Ulianov-Lenin, the catalyst and leader of the Communist Party, considered the Church as the most radical opponent and therefore had to be eliminated. Three major attempts were made to completely annihilate the Orthodox Church in Russia. The first attack was planned and executed by Lenin himself. In December of 1917, he ordered all Church property confiscated, all theological schools closed, outlawed the gathering of Church groups other than for worship, and made civil marriage obligatory (thus, he did not recognize church marriages).

By 1924, the time of Lenin's death, some fifty Bishops were liquidated or deported. Seven hundred priests were either put to death or placed in concentration camps. Patriarch Tikhon of Moscow was imprisoned for a period of time and then released shortly before his death on March 25, 1925. Tikhon designated three Bishops to jointly succeed him as administrators until such time as a new Patriarch could be elected. Two of them died in prison.

The third, Metropolitan Sergius of Novgorod, was also imprisoned and then released March 30, 1927. Upon his release Sergius published a declaration of co-existence which stated: *"We wish to be Orthodox while at the same time recognizing the Soviet Union as our Country. We wish its joys and successes to be our joys and successes and its defeats to be our defeats."* As we shall see a little later in this chapter, many Russian Bishops outside of Russia broke with Moscow as a result of this compromising attitude towards the Communists.

The second attack, instigated by Josif Stalin, came in 1929 when he made it a criminal offense to preach the Gospel, teach religion, argue against communism or atheism, or make any attempt to bring anyone into the Church. While the Christians could still worship, it was under constant surveillience. The bloodbaths, liquidations and banishments to concentration camps began. The second anti-religious wave came to a halt in 1932 when the Communist Government had to turn its attention to the famine and economic difficulties which ensued.

The third and fiercest attack on the Russian Church was made in 1937-1939, when thousands upon thousands of people were uprooted and banished to the extreme north and Siberia. It appeared the Communist Party had finally succeeded, but then the Second World War set in and forced the Communists to bring to a halt their tyranny.

In 1941-1942 the major part of European Russia was overrun by the Germans. Stalin found it necessary to recognize the Church and make a joint appeal to patriotism and nationalism (two things detested by Communism). Metropolitan Sergius and the Russian Church were granted certain freedom. Bishops were returned from exile, and a Synod was convened which elected Sergius as Patriarch of Moscow. Churches were reopened, communities reorganized, theological schools reestablished and religious journals published. However, once the war was over and the Church's usefulness to the State ceased, the Communist attack resumed. Although the bloodbaths of Stalin were no longer apparent, the same fanaticism, persecution and hostility continued until the recent fall of Communism. The Orthodox Church in Russia found it necessary to make an uneasy compromise and tolerate a co-existence with Communism in order to survive. It is very easy for those of us living in a free society to be critical of such a compromise. Still we must be impressed with the fact that in spite of all the violent persecutions for over seventy-five years of Marxist propaganda and totalitarian rule, the Russian Orthodox Church has been able to retain the allegiance of one hundred and three millon Russian Orthodox Christians.

RUSSIAN ORTHODOX CHURCH IN EXILE

A great exodus of Russian exiles took place between 1918 and 1922. The Russian exiles settled mostly in Germany, France and England, where they soon organized themselves into Russian Orthodox Parishes. In 1921 Patriarch Tikhon appointed Metropolitan Evlogy Georgievsky (1894-1946) head of all the Russian Churches in Western Europe. However, when Metropolitan Sergius issued his declaration of peaceful co-existence with the Communist Government on March 30, 1927, the Russian emigres severed their ties with Moscow. In 1931 Metropolitan Evlogy and the Russian Churches in Western Europe entered the jurisdiction of Constantinople.

RUSSIAN ORTHODOX CHURCHES IN AMERICA

The Sitka Diocesan Seat was first transferred to San Francisco and then to New York in 1903. With the Bolshevik Revolution, ties with Moscow were temporarily broken. However, Patriarch Tikhon appointed Metropolitan Plato to head the American Diocese in 1922; but these relations, too, were soon severed as we shall see later. The important point is that with the Communist regime in the Soviet Union, the Russian Orthodox Churches in America split into three groups:

A) RUSSIAN ORTHODOX SYNODAL CHURCH OUTSIDE RUSSIA

The most conservative group is called the Russian Orthodox Synodal Church Outside Russia. This group had its beginning with the Russian emigres in Europe. They perpetuated the hope that the Communist Government would be overthrown and the Tsarist regime reinstated. With Sergius' declaration of peaceful coexistence they completely disassociated themselves with Moscow. Patriarch Tikhon had placed them under Metropolitan Evlogy, who had his seat in Paris. Metropolitan Evlogy placed himself and the emigre Russian Orthodox in Western Europe under the Patriarchate of Constantinople. Some of the Bishops disagreed with Evlogy's action. They also wanted to officially disclaim Sergius' declaration. The Bishops of Western and Eastern Europe gathered at a monastery in Karlovci, Yugoslavia. What resulted from the Karlovci Synod was that one group remained with Evlogy and the other group proclaimed itself as **The Russian Orthodox Synodal Church Outside Russia.**

When Russian emigres from this group came to America they joined forces with the conservative Russians and formed **The Russian Orthodox Synodal Church.** This group came to be the most conservative, regarding themselves the sole spokesmen not only for the Russian Orthodox but for Orthodoxy in general. Holy Trinity Monastery in Jordanville, New York,is the seat, as well as a seminary.

B) RUSSIAN ORTHODOX GREEK CATHOLIC CHURCH OF AMERICAN "METROPOLIA"

The largest of the three Russian groups in America is the Russian Orthodox Greek Catholic Church of America, also formerly known as *"Metropolia."* The *"Metropolia"* succeeded the Russian Diocesan Mission in America after the Bolshevik Revolution 1917-1918. However, in the 1920's all ties with Moscow were severed and the *"Metropolia"* Church declared herself autonomous.

One of the major reasons for *"Metropolia's"* size is that some 85% of her membership are offsprings of immigrants from the former Austro-Hungarian Empire, who were former Uniates. They have two theological schools: St. Tikhon's in Pennsylvania and St. Vladimir's outside New York. In 1970 the *"Metropolia"* petitioned and received autocephalous status from the Patriarchate of Moscow, renaming herself *"Orthodox Church in America."* The Patriarchate of Constantinople did not recognize the autocephaly granted by Moscow because this has always been the prerogative of the Ecumenical Patriarchate. The Greek Orthodox Archdiocese of the Americas recognizes the Orthodox Church in America as a canonical Orthodox Church but does not recognize the autocephaly status. Ultimately the issue will be resolved at the forthcoming Pan-Orthodox Synod which will take place in the next decade or two.

C) THE RUSSIAN ORTHODOX PATRIARCHAL CHURCH

The third and smallest Russian group in America is the Patriarchal Church which remained loyal to Moscow after Sergius' declaration of co-existence. When Moscow granted autocephaly to the Orthodox Church in America, it was presumed that the Patriarchal Churches would embrace the Autochephalous Church. This did not happen. There are still some Moscow Patriarchal Churches in America with a Bishop in New York.

OTHER SLAVIC ORTHODOX CHURCHES

1) AMERICAN CARPATHO-RUSSIA ORTHODOX GREEK CATHOLIC CHURCH

Uniates began migrating to the United States from the nineteenth century. However, many of them, recalling their Orthodox background and the way their ancestors had come under Papal control, started to return to Orthodoxy. These are peoples whose homeland extended along the Carpathian Mountain range (Poland, Czechoslavakia and the Ukraine). During the first two decades of the twentieth century, about one hundred Ukrainian and Carpatho-Russian Uniate Parishes returned to Orthodoxy under the jurisdiction of the Ecumenical Patriarchate of Constantinople.

2) UKRAINIAN ORTHODOX CHURCHES

The Ukrainians are divided into three groups: The Ukrainian Orthodox Church of America, The Ukrainian Orthodox Church of U.S.A. and The Holy Ukrainian Autocephalous Orthodox Church. The first group was organized after the Bolshevik Revolution, while the second group is comprised of the former Uniate Churches referred to in the paragraph above. The first two groups are recognized by all the major Orthodox jurisdictions in America. The third group is not recognized because of some canonical problems regarding the proper ordination of their Bishops.

3) BULGARIAN EASTERN ORTHODOX CHURCH

Before the outbreak of the Macedonian revolution of 1903, there was very little Bulgarian immigration to the United States. Although there were Bulgarian Orthodox Missions, they were not declared a Diocese with a Bishop until 1938. The Patriarchate of Constantinople recognized Sophia as a Bulgarian Patriarchate in 1945. Today there are two Bulgarian Orthodox Churches in America. The one is under the Patriarchate of Bulgaria, and other is under the Orthodox Church in America.

4) SERBIAN ORTHODOX CHURCH

The Serbian Orthodox came to America at the immigration period. The Patriarchate of Belgrade approved the organization of the first Serbian Diocese in America in

1921 and assigned the first Bishop in 1926. Today the Serbians are divided into two groups: The one is under the Patriarchate of Belgrade, and the other is totally independent.

5) ALBANIAN ORTHODOX CHURCH

The Albanians also came to America during the immigration period. Presently there are two Albanian groups in America: The one group is under the Orthodox Church in America, and the other is under the Patriarchate of Constantinople.

6) THE ROMANIAN ORTHODOX CHURCH

The Romanian Orthodox in America is also divided into two groups: One is the Romanian Orthodox Missionary Episcopate in America which is under the Patriarchate of Bucharest, Romania. The other group is under the jurisdiction of the Orthodox Church in America.

7) THE ANTIOCHIAN ORTHODOX CHURCH

The Antiochian Orthodox Church is under the Patriarchate of Antioch and was formerly known as the Syrian Orthodox Church. She was perhaps the first Orthodox Body in America to begin printing service books, religious educational manuals and Orthodox literature and tracts in the English language.

8) THE EVANGELICAL ORTHODOX CHURCH

During the 1960's a group of staff members of Campus Crusade for Christ who were of diverse Protestant backgrounds embarked on a journey which ultimately brought them to the Orthodox Church. They knew their way back to the sixteenth century Protestant Reformation, and all the way back to 95 A.D., the end of the New Testament era. They began a long and tedious biblical, historical, doctrinal, and liturgical search, which ultimately carried them to the historical Eastern Orthodox Church. In 1986 the **Evangelical Orthodox Church** was received into the Patriarchate of Antioch, Syria, and came under the aegis of the Antiochian Orthodox Christian Archdiocese of North America. They have undertaken the challenge to evangelize non-Orthodox Americans and bring them to the Orthodox Church. In a short period of time they have written dozens of books, tracts and pamphlets as well as produced videos on Orthodox teachings and worship.

CONCLUSION

America is an unprecedented phenomena not only for Orthodox Christians, but for Roman Catholics and Protestants as well. Whether in Western Europe, Eastern Europe, the Baltic, Balkan and Middle East States, all Christian Churches were National Churches. If their peoples migrated and/or worked in other areas of the world, they never sought citizenship. It was only in America and Canada where this occurred. The Orthodox who immigrated to America came from National Churches abroad. It was only natural that they would organize under their National Churches. There was no way of foreseeing the divisions which would emerge between the various Orthodox jurisdictions. However, in order to cope and project some type of organic unity, in 1960 **The Standing Conference of Canonical Orthodox Bishops in Americas** (S.C.O.B.A.) was formed. S.C.O.B.A. consists of the leading Bishops of each canonical jurisdiction. It acts as a clearing house to focus the efforts of the Orthodox Church at large on common concerns. Special departments are devoted to college campus, Christian education, military chaplains, regional clergy fellowships, and ecumenical relations.

CHAPTER THIRTY

GREEK ORTHODOX ARCHDIOCESE OF NORTH AND SOUTH AMERICA

As we have seen in the history and tradition of the Orthodox Church, whenever Orthodoxy was introduced into a new territory, country or nation, the Church sent missionaries, clergy and educators to form the skeleton structure of the Church. With the exception of the small missionary effort of the Russian Church in the territory of Alaska and the Aleutian Islands. This did not happen in America; initially even that was intended to be Russian territorial expansion! What actually happened was that pockets of Greek, Russian, Ukrainian, Albanian, Bulgarian, Romanian, Syrian and other Orthodox immigrants settled in various areas of the United States. As each group grew in size, an Orthodox Church emerged. When there were enough churches, they clustered into a Diocese under the jurisdiction of the Orthodox Church in the country or nation of their ethnic background. This is especially the case with the Greek Orthodox Archdiocese of North and South America.

GREEK ORTHODOX CHURCH IN AMERICA

While the first Greek Orthodox Church on the American continent was in New Orleans in 1866, the Greek Orthodox Church in America began in earnest with the Immigration Period from 1890 on. The first church was the Holy Trinity in New York City in 1892. By the end of the first decade of the twentieth century, there were over fifty Greek Orthodox Churches throughout the United States. In the beginning the churches were under the jurisdiction of the Ecumenical Patriarchate of Constantinople. However, in March of 1908 the Patriarchate transferred the jurisdiction of the churches in America over to the Holy Synod of the Orthodox Church Greece. As the number of churches grew, so did the problems of uniformity, discipline and cooperatior become more complex. This was due primarily to the fact that there was no Bishop to shepherd the Greek Orthodox Churches in America. As a result, the clergy had no forum for redress; and the laity assumed a congregational church polity which meant they alone administered and managed the affairs of the church.

POLITICAL PROBLEMS OF GREECE AFFECT GREEK ORTHODOX CHURCHES IN AMERICA

In the early years after the Greek War of Independence, Greece accepted the Bavarian Prince Otto as a plebiscite king. This German bloodline continued through the early twentieth century with King Constantine as monarch during the Turko-Balkan War of 1912. Greece also saw the rise of one of her greatest statesmen in Prime Minister Eleutherios Venizelos. At the outbreak of World War I, Venizelos favored Greece's support of the allies while King Constantine, whose wife was Kaiser Wilhelm's sister, favored neutrality. Venizelos resigned and formed a provisional government in Thessaloniki in 1915. Greece went through a stormy ten-year period with Venizelos and Constantine alternately coming into power.

Greece's political power struggle created havoc on the Greek Orthodox churches in America. The Greek immigrants in America found themselves split into two factions: **Venizelists** and **Royalists.** Unfortunately, the division overflowed into the life of the American churches. Archbishop Theoklitos of Athens was a staunch Royalist and was forced to resign when Venizelos came into power. Archbishop Meletios Metaxakis replaced him and thus was labeled a Venizelist.

Clergy and lay leaders had petitioned both Constantinople and Greece many times to send a bishop to organize their churches along canonical lines and resolve their problems. It was Archbishop Meletios Metaxakis who finally heeded the invitation and request in 1918. After visiting many churches and consulting with many priests and lay leaders. he assigned Bishop Alexander of the Greek See of Rodostolou as Synodical Vicar, over the Greek Churches. However, when Archbishop Meletios returned to Athens, he found he had been deposed because of the return of King Constantine to the throne. Metaxakis returned to America in 1921 and convened a Clergy-Laity Congress in New York City. The Greek Orthodox Archdiocese of North and South America was officially chartered and incorporated in the State of New York. Alexander became the first Archbishop. The official recognition was given by the Ecumenical Patriarchate of Constantinople on May 22, 1922. At the same time, the jurisdiction of the Greek Orthodox churches in America were returned to Constantinople, thus rescinding the 1908 Tome. Regretably the turbulent political events of Greece left indelibly their mark on the Greek immigrants in America —a mark that was to plague the church in America for another three decades.

SYNODIC EXARCHATE OF THE GREEK ORTHODOX CHURCH OF AMERICA

Although the majority of the Greek Orthodox in America came under the jursidiction of the canonical Archdiocese, nonetheless, a small but vocal group of Royalists retained its autonomy. Knowing that Meletios Metaxakis was at the helm of the Archdiocese group, Archbishop Theoklitos of Athens sent Bishop Germanos Traynos of Sparta in July of 1921 to lead the newly-designated Synodic Exarchate of the Greek Orthodox Church of America with headquarters in Lowell, Massachusetts. Thus there emerged two Greek Orthodox Churches in America.

Although the immigrants had come a long way in the new world, they were not skilled in the interpretation of theology and canon law. As a result, they were led by the fervor of their daily emotions. With each new shipload of immigrants the feuding increased, and more communities were established. Additional priests were brought from the homeland, while others were ordained according to their political leanings. In a normal course of growth such events would have been favorable and acceptable. But in these circumstances it was not so because the dissensions grew more intense and more bitter with each passing year.

When Greece returned the jurisdiction of the Church in America to the Ecumenical Throne of Constantinople in 1922, Archbishop Germanos returned to Greece. But his communities remained stubbornly defiant and recalcitrant. They invited Bishop Vasilios Kombopoulos, who was unhappy with his Asia Minor appointment, to become their shepherd. The Synods of Constantinople and Greece jointly suspended him, but he continued with the dissident group. The friction between the two groups heightened in 1924 when both the Ecumenical Patriarchate and the Church of Greece jointly adopted the Gregorian Calendar. The Julian Calendar was introduced by Julius Ceasar in 46 B.C., and was used until it was corrected in 1582. Since the correction was introduced during the time of Pope Gregory XIII, it is called the Gregorian Calendar. The canonical Archdiocese accepted the calendar change while the Royalists kept the Julian Calendar. They came to be known as the *"Palaio [Old] Emeroloyites [Calendarists]"*. A small number of Old Calendarist churches still exists until the present, primarily in the New York area.

BISHOP DAMASKENOS, METROPOLITAN OF CORINTH

In 1930 Patriarch Photios II, in collaboration with Archbishop Chrysostomos Papadopoulos of Athens, decided to solve the canonical problem in America once and for all. Papadopoulos was professor of canon law at the University of Athens and had accompanied Meletios Metaxakis on his 1918 trip to America. Therefore he had firsthand knowledge of the dilemma. The two prelates dispatched Bishop Damaskenos of Corinth to assume temporary administration of all the Greek Orthodox Churches, canonical and dissident. His charge was to make an in-depth study, reconcile the disputing factions and make concrete recommendations to both the Ecumenical Patriarchate and the Holy Synod of Greece.

When Bishop Damaskenos arrived in New York on May 20, 1930, the Archdiocese had 133 churches and the Autocephalous group had 50. Damaskenos' arrival precipitated a variety of reactions. Some looked to him as a messiah while others looked at his arrival with suspicion and apprehension. After careful study Damaskenos made the following recommendations:

1) Archbishop Alexander, his assisting bishops and Bishop Vasilios Kombopoulos return to Athens for new assignments.

2) The Archdiocese with four Synodal Bishops (New York, Chicago, Boston and San Francisco) be temporarily dissolved. The Archdiocese has one Archbishop and four assisting Bishops for the four Diocesan Districts. This temporary solution was intended to facilitate the reconciliation and reunification of the parishes, and remained in effect until 1974.

3) The Ecumenical Patriarchate and the Holy Synod of Greece jointly approve the appointment of a new hierarch --one steeped in Orthodox theologial tradition, fluent in English, and possessing great patience and exemplary diplomacy.

ARCHBISHOP ATHENAGORAS (1930-1948)

The Metropolitan Bishop of Corfu, Athenagoras Spyrou, the new Archbishop of the Greek Orthodox Archdiocese of North and South America, arrived in New York on February 14, 1931. During his hierarchal tenure he brought most of the dissident churches back to the Archdiocese. He founded new parishes, the Ladies Philoptochos

Societies, Holy Cross Seminary (first in Pomphret, Connecticut, and then in Brookline, Massachusetts), Saint Basil's Care Center for Children and Girls Academy (Garrison, New York), the Orthodox Observer (monthly publication) and Mission Churches in Latin and South America. On November 1, 1948, Archbishop Athenagoras was elected Ecumenical Patriarch of Constantinople. He died at the age of 86 on July 7, 1972. He was succeeded by Demetrios I, who was succeeded by Bartholomaios I. Patriarch Bartholomaios holds that office until the present.

ARCHBISHOP MICHAEL (1949-1958)

Metropolitan Michael Constantinides, Bishop of Corinth, succeeded Athenagoras and remained as Archbishop of the Americas until his death on July 13, 1958. A brilliant scholar and linguist, steeped in the theology of St. Paul and St. Athanasius the Great, Archbishop Michael greatly enhanced the prestige of Orthodox Christianity in America. In addition to his administrative achievements he founded the Greek Orthodox Youth of America, the "Home for the Aged" (Yonkers, N.Y.), promoted national recognition of Eastern Orthodoxy as a major faith in America, created a Public Relations Department, joined the National Council of Churches in America, became one of the five presidents of the World Council of Churches Presidium, and was the first Orthodox Prelate to deliver an invocation at a presidential inauguration (Dwight D. Eisenhower, January 1957). The late Archbishop Michael was laid to rest in a special place on the grounds of St. Basil's Academy, Garrison, N.Y.

ARCHBISHOP IAKOVOS (1959-1996)

Archbishop Iakovos arrived in the United States in 1939. He served parishes in Hartford, St. Louis and Boston. He also served Dean of Holy Cross Seminary. He was elected and enthroned Archbishop of America April 1, 1959.

Archbishop Iakovos was instrumental in reshaping American Orthodoxy and was considered the most influential Orthodox Prelate in America. At his initiative the Archdiocese was restructured and chartered as a Synodal Church in 1974. Archbishop Iakovos retired July 29, 1996 and was succeeded by Archbishop Spyridon September of 1997.

ARCHBISHOP SPYRIDON (1997-Present)

Archbishop Spyridon was born in the United States. He graduated from the Patriarchal Seminary of Halki. After serving in various capacities in Italy he was elevated to the rank of Metropolitan of Italy. Shortly after the retirment of Archbishop Iakovos, Spyridon was elected Archbishop of the Greek Orthodox Archdiocese of America. He serves in that office until the present.

CONCLUSION

This chapter has attempted to trace the Greek Orthodox Church in America from its earliest beginnings, through its most trying and difficult period of adjustment, to its present position. As has been noted, the Greek communicants, as immigrants and Eastern Orthodox Christians, had an historical beginning in America which was quite unique. That uniqueness has proven to be a strength and weakness: weakness in that the structural and organizational adjustment was slow; strength in its tenacity and fortitude to persist in spite of great odds and obstacles to adjust to the American way of life and yet hold on to a religious persuasion and cultural heritage.

The ultimate question, in the final analysis, is whether the Greek Orthodox Church will survive in America. Will the sociological forces so prevalent in America draw us into the assimilation process? Or to put it another way, will the Orthodox Church be pulled into the Anglo-Saxon melting pot and be synthesized to the extent of being extinct? Hellenistic culture flavored and influenced the

Early Christian Church and continued doing so through the Patristic Age, Medieval Period and Middle Ages, at least in the lands where Orthodoxy prevailed. It is that element which is found in Orthodox theology, tradition and worship that will not lose its entity nor its identity. Rather than **assimilate** into the various and sundry American religious denominations, we must **integrate** twenty centuries of the Orthodox Christian Faith into the American world and American life. What is more, it will grow and contribute to the mainstream of religion and nationalism in America. The historical conditions at the turn of the century, the Venizelist/Royalist controversy, the disorganization and disunity of our churches, as well as the dissensions each illustrates vividly why our Church in America took so long to mature. To make blanket condemnations of the Greek immigrants is to completely ignore the obstacles and difficulties they encountered, endured and overcame. We must bear in mind that the immigrant Greek had no intentions of remaining in America. Therefore, it is plain to see that his interest in Greek politics was a genuine one. They thought of themselves as temporary residents, grateful to be here, but convinced that their sojourn was not permanent —that they would eventually return to Greece. By the time the Second World War broke out, they fully realized that America was their home; and most became American citizens. They also knew that the Greek Orthodox Church was here to stay!

It would be a great injustice and a distortion of the truth to leave the impression that the Church was just a political arena. The vast majority of clergy and laity in the Greek Orthodox churches in America were dedicated and faithful Orthodox Christians. They may have lacked the educational background most of us, their offspring, have; but theirs was a worshipping faith that is worthy of praise and emulation. Whatever we have today is a result of their efforts, their labors and their strong convictions. Let us hope that this generation and those to come will live up to the same ideals. There are not enough words to extol the virtues and achievements of those men and women immigrants. Truly, they were giants!

CHAPTER THIRTY-ONE

THE ORTHODOX CHURCH AND THE ECUMENICAL MOVEMENT

An Orthodox Christian may approach the Ecumenical Movement by seeing its roots in the formation of Israel in history. God has created for Himself a people with the mission of uniting humanity in the true worship of God and eternal coexistence in God's love, grace, countenance and glory. Adam and Eve broke the Covenant Promise of God by their own choice and turned away from their own true purpose and destination. But God was not satisfied to merely let them die with no hope. Therefore, He restated the Covenant Promise (Oral) to Abraham and restored it to Abraham's grandson, Jacob. Jacob was renamed Israel, *The Chosen One*, and all his descendents became Israelites, *The Chosen Ones of God*. With the passing of time, the Israelites found the Covenant Promise difficult to adhere to and found pagan religions, ungodly practices and sin more tempting. God found it necessary to give them the Covenant Promise in a tangible way --The Written Covenant, The Ten Commandments!

Still the Israelites strayed! Even in spite of God's persistent reminders through His prophets and holy men. But God is a God Who will not let His people go. Finally, God found it necessary to come Himself, in the Person of Jesus Christ, in order to reconcile and unite all mankind into One Universal Israelite (Chosen) Nation of God. Jesus Christ accomplished this through His Crucifixion (Blood Covenant) and His Triumphant Resurrection over sin, evil, corruption and death!

Since the Jews of Jesus' time rejected Him and His Holy Church, Orthodox theology believes that the Christian Church is the *New Israel*, the New Zion, the New Jerusalem. The Patriarchs, Prophets and Saints of the Old Testament, and the Apostles, Martyrs and Saints of the

New Testament are ever-present living witnesses in the worship and piety of Orthodox Christians. Moreover, Orthodox Christians believe themselves to be, by virtue of Baptism, Chrismation and the Eucharist, along with the other Sacraments and liturgical experiential worship, members of this One Universal Chosen Nation of God.

THE CHRISTIAN CHURCH

Christianity appeared on the scene during the period of the Roman Empire under the cultural forces of Hellenistic Civilization. Out of the fusion of the Greco-Roman and Judeo-Christian cultures, the roots of Western Civilization were sprung. During the first three centuries of church history Christians considered themselves as members of a separate nation --a society apart, yet a society within the Greco-Roman world. Following the Edict of Toleration in 313 A.D., however, the picture changed drastically and dramatically. With the freedom given to the Christians, a multiplicity of peoples were united religiously, socially and politically: Goths, Huns, Scandinavians, Anglo-Saxons, Germans, Slavs, Tatars and Gauls, just to name a few. What took place was a fusion of culture, heritage, environment and faith in Jesus Christ which resulted into one United Christian Church. This was the first indication of Ecumenism. As New Nations and States emerged, the Christian Church developed her dogmas and established forms for worship and policies for administration through both Local and Ecumenical Councils.

THE POSITION OF THE BISHOP OF ROME

In the Ancient Church each area was headed by a Bishop. The Bishops organized themselves into Synods or Councils. Since the Roman Empire had been divided into Provinces and subdivided into Districts, it was only natural for the Church to adopt the same divisions. Therefore, it became the practice for Bishops of larger cities to preside at Councils and accorded a *primacy of honor.* There was also a higher scale of *primacy of honor* for those Bishops of imperial cities and capitals: Rome, Alexandria, Antioch, Jerusalem and Constantinople. Up to the fourth century Rome was accorded the highest *primacy of honor.* When Constantinople became the capital, the Second Ecumenical Council (381 A.D.) called her *New Rome* and gave her Bishop equal *primacy of honor* with the Bishop of Old Rome.

With the transfer of the capital of the Roman Empire to the East political, economic and social order disintegrated in the West. With the decline and decay came a weakening of imperial central authority. By the latter part of the fourth century the Bishop of Rome began to emerge as the central authority to whom Tribal States in the West looked for guidance and direction. As the Bishop of Rome began to assume the role of temporal ruler, it was natural for the Papacy to react strongly against the counciliar canon granting equal *primacy of honor to New Rome* (Constantinople).

Later centuries brought the Feudal System which penetrated all the aspects of the Church in the West. With its political theories it shaped the administrative principles in Western Canon Law, which in turn had a tremendous impact on the evolution of Papal Authority. The appointment by the German and Frankish Emperors of Bishops to be Vassal Lords over the domains of the Holy Roman Empire of the Germans led to the control and corruption of the ancient practice of autonomy (self-government).

EAST AND WEST CONFLICT

The Eastern Bishops and theologians noted the distortion of doctrines in the West, but somehow they hoped they would be corrected. However, when Pope Nicholas (858-867) attempted to intervene in Patriarch Photios'

(858-867 and 877-886) enthronement and asserted his Papal claims of authority over the entire Christian Church, then he violated the cardinal rule of autonomy which had been respected and preserved in both the East and West from ancient times.

The second conflict came when Pope Leo IX (1048-1054) sent Cardinal Humbert, Archbishop Frederick of Lorraine and Bishop Peter of Amalfi to Constantinople with a letter demanding papal claims be respected and obeyed. When Patriarch Michael Cerularios (1043-1058) refused the intervention, the three delegates from Rome issued the Bull of Excommunication on July 6, 1054. Patriarch Michael Cerularios, in consort with the Patriarchs of Antioch, Jerusalem and Alexandria mutually excommunicated the Pope of Rome. What had once been the **One, Holy, Catholic and Apostolic Church** became separated into the Church of the East and the Church of the West. The Church of the East included the Ancient Patriarchates of Constantinople, Jerusalem, Antioch and Alexandria; the National Churches of the Ukraine, Russia, Bulgaria, Yugoslavia, Romania, Greece, Cyprus and the Balkan Countries; and those in the Middle East and Asia Minor (present day Turkey). This Church today remains united and is known as the **Eastern Orthodox Church.** On the other hand, the Church of the West, the **Roman Catholic Church,** which included Western Europe under the Patriarchate of Rome, remained united until the sixteenth century when the first of many separations began with the Protestant Reformation. It seemed that the One, Holy, Catholic and Apostolic Church had reached a point of no return, that there would never come a time when the Churches could unite in any form whatever. Many years passed; but with the turn of the twentieth century, the Christian Churches entered into a new spirit of Christian love, which evolved into informal meetings that we know today as *Ecumenism* and the *Ecumenical Movement*.

THE PATRIARCHATE OF CONSTANTINOPLE AND THE ECUMENICAL MOVEMENT

What role has the Ecumenical Patriarchate of Constantinople played in the Ecumenical Movement? In 1902 the Ecumenical Patriarch issued a Synodical Encyclical addressed to the Patriarchs of Alexandria, Jerusalem and Antioch, and to the Heads of the Autocephalous Churches of Cyprus, Russia, Greece and Montenegro (Yugoslavia and Albania). It contained a reference to discuss the possibility of an Ecumenical Movement. Later, in 1920, the Ecumenical Patriarchate of Constantinople issued a call to all leaders of Christianity throughout the World, asking them to come to a closer relationship with each other in Christian Unity. This encyclical was entitled: *"Unto All the Churches of Christ Wheresoever They Be."* The encyclical suggested a *League of Nations* type of structure form that would lead to what later followed as *Faith and Order Dialogue*. Specifically, it stated:

"And this friendship and kindly disposition towards each other can, to our mind, be demonstrated and more especially proved in the following manner:

a) By the acceptance of a uniform calendar, for the simultaneous celebration of all the great Christian Feasts by all the Churches. [The Gregorian Calendar was subsequently adopted in 1924 by the Patriarchate of Constantinople and the Church of Greece.]

b) By the exchange of brotherly letters on the great Feasts of the ecclesiastical year, when it is customary to do so, and on other exceptional occasions.

c) By a more friendly meeting between the representatives of the various Churches, wherever they may be.

d) By an interrelation between Theological Schools and

the representatives of theological science, and by the exchange of theological students between seminaries of all different Churches.

e) By convening Pan-Christian Conferences to examine questions of a common interest to all Churches.

f) By the impartial and in a more historical way examination of the doctrinal differences both from the chair and in theological treatises.

g) By mutually respecting the customs and usages prevailing in each Church.

h) By allowing to each other the use of places of prayer and of cemeteries for the funeral and burial of persons belonging to other confessions dying in foreign lands.

i) By the settlement of the questions of mixed marriages between the various confessions.

j) And finally, by the mutual support of the Churches in the work of strengthening religious beliefs, of charity and the like.

This encyclical was written in 1920. Compare it with the *Faith and Order Dialogue* Meetings in Lausanne, Switzerland in 1927; Edinburgh, England in 1937; and the ultimate formation of the World Council of Churches in Amsterdam, Holland, in 1948. Since that time there have been World Council of Churches Meetings every seven years. The Orthodox Church has been a ready participant at each meeting. In fact, the presence of Orthodox theologians prevents the World Council of Churches from appearing to be simply a Pan-Protestant Alliance.

While the World Council of Churches has played a great role in bringing Orthodox and Protestants together, there are some conservative Orthodox who think we should not be members. This is especially true in the past twenty years or so, when some Protestant theologians have attempted to integrate and reconcile representatives of non-Trinitarian theology, liberation theology and Far Eastern Religions into the Trinitarian milieu of the World Council of Churches. Nevertheless, the presence and participation of the Orthodox Churches in the World Council of Churches offers a two-thousand-years-old witness of the True Faith delivered from Christ through the Apostles and the Patristic Fathers.

INTERFAITH DIALOGUE

The Orthodox Church, through her hierarchs and theologians,has been engaged in Interfaith Dialogue since the First World War. This Dialogue is on several levels.For example, Orthodox theologians and theologians of the Oriental Churches (Armenians, Egyptians, Ethiopians and other Monophysite Churches)have met repeatedly and are coming very close to a union. While the Roman Catholic Church is not a member of the World Council of Churches, nevertheless, International Dialogue (Between Rome and Constantinople) and National Dialogue (America) have been going on for over twenty years. The Orthodox Church is in dialogue with theologians of Judaism and Islam. In addition, the Orthodox Church is in dialogue with Lutherans, Anglicans, Baptists, Methodists and Pentecostalists.

CONCLUSION

Many advancements have been made and more are in sight between Orthodox, Roman Catholics and Protestants. However, we must be very careful not to mistake genuine rapproachement to Christian **Unity** with easy footsteps to **Union.** Christian Unity can be achieved in common sympathy,common problems, common issues, in understanding each other, appreciating each others' contributions, respecting each others' convictions and drawing from each others' resources. But the Orthodox Church thinks it a fallacy to mistakenly confuse the word **Unity** for **Union.** Union presents many stumbling blocks that will require serious-minded and sober theological deliberations. Christian Unity is the function and the role of the World Council of Churches. Christian Union will require much more!

THE ORTHODOX CHRISTIAN VIEW OF REUNION

What does the Orthodox Church seek in Christian Union? It does not seek a **Return to Rome**, nor a **Return to Byzantium**, nor to **Luther and Calvin**! The Orthodox attitude concerning **Return** is not an appeal to the other Churches to return within the historical structure of the Orthodox Church. Rather, it is an appeal to all Churches to find ***their* Orthodoxy** in ***themselves.*** They must return to the Tradition, Doctrine, Ecclesiology and Liturgical Experiential Worship of the **One, Holy, Catholic and Apostolic Church** from which they all sprang and which does not allow them to remain separate. It means a return to the ***"Phronema ton Pateron,"*** to the religious, spiritual and doctrinal attitude and position of the Fathers of the Patristic Era.

If the Orthodox Church has appeared static, it is due to historical, not organic reasons. A Church which produces learned theologians and good Christians in peace time only is less entitled to be called a **Living Church** than one that fights for the Christian Faith, nurtures and inspires Martyrs and Saints, and great clouds of witnesses. This is what the Orthodox Church did through four hundred fifty years of Ottoman Subjugation. This is what the Orthodox Christians behind the Iron Curtain have been doing for over seven decades. **The Orthodox Church is a Living Church!** She has been and will continue to be so!

EPILOGUE

The author of this history book has repeatedly stated that it is his personal contention and conviction that the Orthodox Church has a tremendous contribution to make on the American scene. He has emphasized over and over the importance of having a scriptural, historical, doctrinal, traditional and liturgical background of the **One, Holy, Catholic and Apostolic Church.** He has attempted to present in an objective way the history and development of the differences which led to the Great Schism in 1054, through the major divisions, up to the present time. The responsibility remains the same throughout: You, the student of history must evaluate and draw your own concusions. But there is a great challenge, too, to learn, discern, experience and pass on the True Faith!

During the Sacrament of Ordination in the Orthodox Church a very unique act takes place. Once the priest has been ordained and fully vested, the Divine Liturgy continues where it left off. After the consecration of the Holy Gifts, the Bishop places the Communion *Amnos* (consecrated Body of Christ) into the clasped hands of the newly-ordained priest and has him stand at the Crucifix, beind the holy altar table. He charges him with the following words:

> ***"Receive this deposit and vigilantly watch over it until the Second Coming of our Lord Jesus Christ, at which time from Him it shall be asked of you!"***

Accept ***Your*** Orthodox Baptism as a **deposit** and watch over it **vigilantly** with a Eucharistic, Sacramental and Christlike life. Thus knowing that Jesus Christ will ask each of us for an accounting of our actions, deeds and thoughts. Treasure and live Your **Orthodox Christian Faith!**

BIBLIOGRAPHY AND RECOMMENDED READING

Althaus, Paul, *Theology of Martin Luther.*
Bainton, Roland, *Reformation of the Sixteenth Century.*
Baynes, Norman and Moss, L., *Byzantium.*
Bensen, Basil, *Russian Orthodox Church in Alaska: 1794-1967.*
Cavarnos, Constantine, *Byzantine Sacred Music and Icon.*
Byzantine Thought and Art.
Chrysostom, Bishop and Hieromonk Auxentios,
Scripture and Tradition.
Coniaris, Anthony, *Introducing the Orthodox Church.*
Diehl, Charles, *Byzantium: Greatness and Decline.*
Dillenberger, John, *Martin Luther.*
Efthimiou, Miltiades,
History of the Greek Orthodox Church in America.
Hughs, Philip, *Popular History of the Roman Catholic Church.*
Haussy, H.W., History of Byzantine Civilization.
Fedetov, G.P., *Treasury of Russian Spirituality.*
Fletcher, William C.,
Russian Orthodox Church Underground: 1917-1970.
Florovsky, Georges,
Bible, Church and Tradition.
Christianity and Culture.
Creation and Redemption.
The Ways of Russian Theology.
Fouyos, Methodios,
Orthodoxy, Roman Catholicism and Anglicanism.
Frangopoulos, Athanasios, *Our Orthodox Christian Faith.*
Gavin, Frank, *Some Aspects of Contemporary Greek Thought.*
Geanokoplos, Deno, *Byzantine East and Latin West.*
Byzantium.
Gillquist, Peter, *Becoming Orthodox.*
Harakas, Stanley,
The Orthodox Church: 455 Questions and Answers.
Contemporary Moral Issues.
Hudson, Winthrop, *Religions in America.*
Kanoutas, Serafim, *Greeks in America.*
Karanicolas, Panteleimon, *The Protestants.*
Kavadas, Athenagoras, *History of Protestantism.*

Knox, Ronald, *Beliefs* of *Roman Catholics.*
Kokkinakis, Athenagoras,
The Thyateira Confession.
Koulomzin, Sophie, *Orthodox Church Through the Ages.*
Kourides, Peter T.,
Evolution of the Greek Orthodox Church in America.
Latourette, Kenneth Scott, *A History of Christianity.*
Lossky, Vladimir, *Introduction to Orthodox Theology.*
Meaning of Icons.
Lindsay,Thomas, *History of the Reformation.*
Mastrantonis, George, *New-Style Catechism on the Eastern Orthodox Faith for Adults.*
Malafouris, Bobby, *Greeks in America.*
Mead, S. Frank, *Handbook of Denominations.*
Meyendorff, John, *Byzantine Theology.*
Catholicity and the Church.
Living Tradition.
The Orthodox Church.
Moschos, Charles, *Greek Americans.*
Ostrogorsky, George, *History of the Byzantine Empire.*
Ouspensky, Leonid, *Theology of the Icon.*
Papaioannou,George, *Odyssey of Hellenism in America.*
Patelos, Constantine, *The Orthodox Church in the Ecumenical Movement.*
Runciman, Steven, *The Eastern Schism.*
History of the Crusades.
Fall of Constantinople.
The Great Church in Captivity.
Saloutos, Theodore, *Greeks in the United States.*
Schaff, Philip, *History of the Christian Church.*
Schmemann, Alexander, *Historical Road to Orthodoxy.*
Of Water and Spirit.
Introduction to Liturgical Theology.
The Idea of Primacy in Eastern Ecclesiology.
Staniloae, Dumitru, *Theology and the Church.*
Stephanides, Vasilios, *Church History.*
Stroyan, William, *Communist Russia and the Russian Orthodox Church: 1943-1962.*

Troeltsch, Ernst, *Protestantism and Progress.*
Vasiliev, A.A., *The Byzantine Empire.*
Ward, A.W., *The Counter Reformation.*
Ware, Timothy, *The Orthodox Church.*
The Orthodox Way.
Zernov, Nicholas, *Eastern Christendom.*
The Russians and Their Church.
Zoustis, Vasilios,
Greeks in America and Their Activities.

HISTORICAL CHART

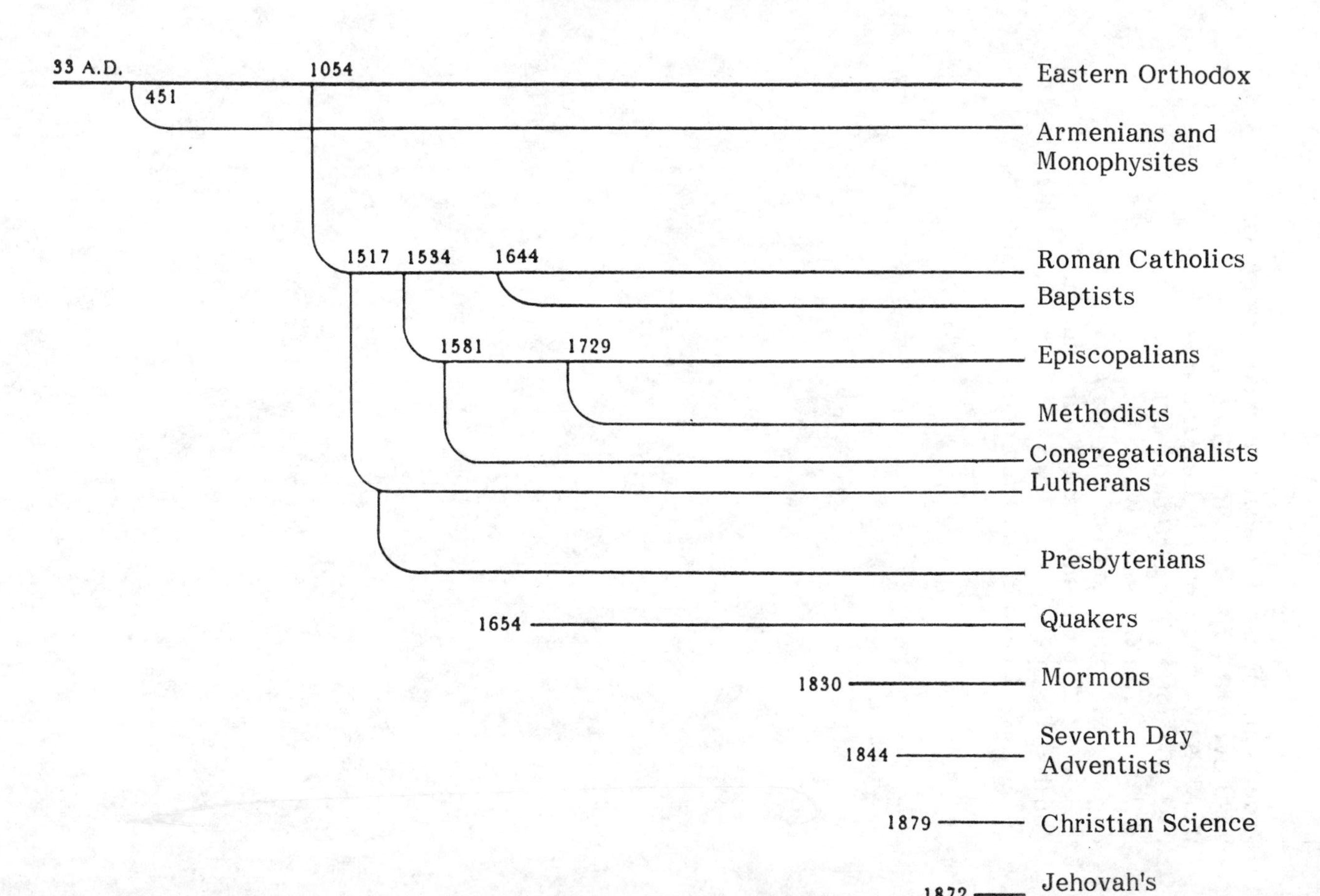